Lab Manual

to accompany

Data Structures and
Abstractions with Java™
SECOND EDITION

Frank M. Carrano

Charles Hoot
Oklahoma City University

PEARSON
Prentice
Hall

W9-CNA-503

Upper Saddle River, NJ 07458

Vice President and Editorial Director, ECS: *Marcia J. Horton*
Executive Editor: *Tracy Dunkelberger*
Associate Editor: *Carole Snyder*
Editorial Assistant: *Christianna Lee*
Executive Managing Editor: *Vince O'Brien*
Managing Editor: *Camille Trentacoste*
Manufacturing Manager, ESM: *Alexis Heydt-Long*
Manufacturing Buyer: *Lisa McDowell*
Executive Marketing Manager: *Robin O'Brien*
Marketing Assistant: *Mack Patterson*

© 2007 Pearson Education, Inc.
Pearson Prentice Hall
Pearson Education, Inc.
Upper Saddle River, NJ 07458

Pearson Prentice Hall™ is a trademark of Pearson Education, Inc.
All other tradmarks or product names are the property of their respective owners.

The author and publisher of this book have used their best efforts in preparing this book. These efforts include the development, research, and testing of the theories and programs to determine their effectiveness. The author and publisher make no warranty of any kind, expressed or implied, with regard to these programs or the documentation contained in this book. The author and publisher shall not be liable in any event for incidental or consequential damages in connection with, or arising out of, the furnishing, performance, or use of these programs.

ISBN 0-13-615619-3

Pearson Education Ltd., *London*
Pearson Education Australia Pty. Ltd., *Sydney*
Pearson Education Singapore, Pte. Ltd.
Pearson Education North Asia Ltd., *Hong Kong*
Pearson Education Canada, Inc., *Toronto*
Pearson Educación de Mexico, S.A. de C.V.
Pearson Education—Japan, *Tokyo*
Pearson Education Malaysia, Pte. Ltd.
Pearson Education, Inc., *Upper Saddle River, New Jersey*

Table of Contents

Preface

Introduction

In general, the labs in this manual are designed to give you some experience in using and implementing data structures.

A number of the labs ask you to complete a program that uses a particular data structure. You will find as you continue programming that the data structures you learn in this course will be the primary tools in your programming tool kit. These labs should serve as an intermediate step in your programming life. Before you do the lab, it is your responsibility to study carefully the concepts and code for the particular structure. The lab will then give you support and direction for finishing an application. It is important not to stop there, but to write other programs of your own that use the data structure.

The other labs ask you to work on the implementation of a data structure. Other programmers, however, have already implemented the common data structures and it would be foolish to rewrite them each time you need them. So why do labs that work with the implementations? There are two main reasons. The first reason is that it will help you understand the performance of the particular data structure better. The second reason is that you may find the existing data structures do not quite match your needs. As you create a new data structure or modify an existing data structure, your practice with the techniques shown in this lab manual will be helpful.

Before going on, I must mention a few things that this manual is not designed to do.

- This manual is not intended to teach you how to design programs. It is presumed that you have already spent time learning the basic techniques of decomposing a problem and can write an algorithm to accomplish a task.

- This manual is not intended to teach you how to write programs. Again, this should have been covered in your previous course work. You should be well familiar with all the basic programming constructs like iteration and be able to write methods to accomplish tasks. It is also assumed that you have familiarity with the basic mechanics of how objects work.

- This manual is not intended to teach you how to program in Java. If you know C/C++, you will find that there are a number of similarities to Java. In many ways Java is a friendlier language, but there are enough differences that it is not advisable for this to be your first experience using Java. In particular, one of the major differences is in the details of how Java deals with objects and classes. Every lab will use classes.

- This manual is not intended to teach you how to design object-oriented programs. How to divide the responsibilities of a program between cooperating objects is the subject of a semester long course that often comes after data structures. The programs in these labs have been created with object-oriented design principles in mind and hopefully will foreshadow that material.

Structure of the Labs

All of the labs follow the same structure:

1. Goal
2. Resources
3. Java Files
4. Introduction
5. Pre-Lab Visualization

6. Directed Lab Work

7. Post-Lab Follow-Ups

The Goal is a concise explanation of the purpose of the lab. In the Resources you will find references to key chapters in *Data Structures and Abstractions with Java (Second Edition)* by Carrano. Before you start the lab, it is hoped that you have read that material first. In addition, files or relevant hyperlinks may be given. The Java Files section lists all the files that you will use in the lab. The Introduction provides supplementary material to that in your book where needed and introduces you to the specifics of the material covered in the lab. The Pre-Lab Visualization gives a number of exercises intended to help you think about the problem and prepare to write the code. You should do these exercises before doing any work at a computer. This kind of preparatory work is a good habit to get into and will increase the quality of your code. The next section contains the instructions for the lab. In general, you will be asked to complete the code iteratively. You will write code to do a small task, and then test to see that it works. Again, this is a recommended habit to cultivate. The post-lab section gives exercises that invite you to reflect on what you have done or that extend the work that you have done in the lab.

Java Environments

One of the advantages of working with Java is that platform issues are minimized. Whether you are using a workstation or a personal computer should not matter. Having said that, you have a number of choices of environments for developing programs in Java.

The simplest choice is to use an editor and then compile and run your programs from the command line. While this is a classic technique, more support can be had. These more advanced environments may offer program composition tools, visualization tools, compilation tools, version tools, automatic code generation tools, and debugging tools. This manual is not written for any specific environment, and which one you use will depend on your resources.

There are two online resources that you might find useful. The first is java.sun.com. This is the starting point for all things Java. Here you can find free downloads like Java 2 Platform, Standard Edition, and NetBeans. You can also find tutorials and documentation for Java. One useful starting point is the Application Program Interface (API) documentation that documents all of the standard classes and their methods. At the time this was written, the most recent version of Java was 1.5.0 and the API documentation was at java.sun.com/j2se/1.5.0/docs/api/. Please refer to the Java Website for the most recent version.

The second is www.bluej.org. BlueJ is an integrated development environment designed for teaching. It can be downloaded for free. One of the nice features BlueJ has is the ability to create objects and then invoke methods on those objects. This can be an aid in debugging classes.

Conclusion

The course on data structures is one of the critical courses in computer science. It is usually the first course that ties together the theoretical mathematics that underpins computer science with the practical aspects of writing programs in a systematic way. I have found that it is a key indicator of the performance of students in upper-division undergraduate work and beyond. The better you understand this material, the better you will do later. I wish you every success and hope that this manual helps you.

Sincerely,

Dr. Charles Hoot

Note to Instructors

These labs were designed with the intention that students would do the Pre-Lab Exercises before the lab session. The lab session would then be an opportunity for the student to work with guidance from an instructor. To make sure that students are on the right track, it may be helpful to check their Pre-Lab Exercises before the start of lab.

Due to time constraints, it may not be possible for students to complete the entire directed lab within one lab session. (This becomes a certainty if they don't do the Pre-Lab beforehand.) In such cases, a portion of the lab can be made the focus of the lab session and the remaining parts either skipped or given as a take-home assignment.

Lab 1   Objects

Goal

In this lab you will explore constructing and testing an object.

Resources

- Chapter 1: Java Classes
- Chapter 2: Creating Classes from Other Classes
- Chapter 3: Designing Classes
- Rational.html—Interface documentation for the class Rational
- Counter.html—Interface documentation for the class Counter

Java Files

- Rational.java
- ZeroDenominatorException.java
- RationalTest.java
- Counter.java
- CounterTest.java

Introduction

Before you build a class, you should determine what its responsibilities are. Responsibilities express the duties of an object in its interactions with other objects. Some typical kinds of responsibilities are knowing, computing, controlling, and interacting with a user. For example, consider a class representing a bank account. It would have a responsibility to know the balance of the account. An accessor method that returns the value of a private variable holding the balance can fulfill that responsibility. Another responsibility of the bank account class might be to compute the monthly interest. That responsibility can be fulfilled by a mutator method that first computes the interest and then modifies the balance. But who decides when the interest should be computed? This is an example of a controller responsibility and most likely would not be the responsibility of the bank account class. Suppose you wished to withdraw a hundred dollars from your account. What class would be responsible for doing the input and output? Again, it is probably not the bank account class. The interface could be an automated teller, a Java program running on the web, or even just a plain terminal. If the bank account class is responsible for the interaction, it will be susceptible to frequent changes as different technologies are developed and used to allow a customer to interact with his or her account. To protect the bank account from those kinds of changes, the interaction responsibility will be assigned to other classes that have interaction as their primary responsibility. The classes that will be developed in this lab manual are intended to be very general and therefore will usually not have any interaction responsibilities. Deciding which responsibilities a class should have is a design issue that is the province of a course on object-oriented programming. To do it well takes practice.

Once the responsibilities of a class have been determined, an implementation is designed to meet those responsibilities. The implementation will consist of two pieces: the variables whose values comprise the state of the object, and the methods that comprise the protocol for the class. But when is the implementation correct? The answer to this question is addressed in two ways.

The first approach is the use of invariants. As a class is being designed, look for constraints (invariants) on the state of the object that should always be true. For example, consider the bank account class. One invariant might be that the interest rate should always be greater than or equal to zero. Another invariant could be that the balance should always be the total amount deposited minus the total amount withdrawn. One of the primary functions of the constructor is to start the object in a valid state. (All invariants are true.) Mutator methods (those that change the state) should guarantee that they leave the object in a valid state.

But this is not enough. Suppose that the bank account class has a deposit method. If that method was invoked with a thousand dollars, but it only added a hundred dollars to the total deposits and the balance, it would meet the invariant. Unfortunately, the bank would have some very unhappy customers. The second approach is to ensure the correct operation of the methods. Besides guaranteeing that the state is valid after the method completes, it must be the correct state. Additionally, any value returned by the method must be correct. There are other ways to specify the correct operation of methods, but pre- and post-conditions are very common. Pre-conditions specify what the method expects to be true before it is invoked. Post-conditions specify what must be true after the method is invoked provided that the pre-conditions were met. For example, consider a deposit method for the bank account class:

```
deposit (int amount)
```

What are the pre-conditions? Certainly the bank account must be in a valid state, but is there anything else? Can the deposit be negative? No. This suggests a pre-condition that the amount must be non-negative. The client has the responsibility to guarantee that the pre-condition is met. What happens if the object's client makes a mistake and accidentally invokes the method with a negative value? There are two ways of handling the situation. The first technique is to be safe and test for the pre-condition. If it is not met, the state of the object will be unchanged and an error will be thrown. With the second technique, instead of having the requirement in the pre-conditions, it will be part of the post-conditions. A Boolean return value is added to the deposit method and if the amount is negative, the state will be unchanged and false will be returned. Otherwise, the total deposits will be increased by amount, the balance will be increased by amount, and true will be returned.

It should be mentioned that besides pre- and post-conditions, another way of specifying the behavior of a class is via the use of test code. While test cases are an important tool and these labs will use them extensively, do not become overly reliant on them. Passing the test cases does not guarantee that the class is behaving correctly.

In today's lab, you will work with two classes. The first class will represent a rational number that is the ratio of two integer values. The second class will be a counter that has both a minimum and maximum value.

Pre-Lab Visualization

Rational

Here is a list of responsibilities for the rational class:

1. Know the value of the denominator.
2. Know the value of the numerator.
3. Be able to compute the negation of a rational number.
4. Be able to compute the reciprocal of a rational number.
5. Be able to compare two rational numbers for equality.
6. Be able to compute the sum of two rational numbers.
7. Be able to compute the difference of two rational numbers.
8. Be able to compute the result of multiplying two rational numbers.
9. Be able to compute the result of dividing two rational numbers.
10. Be able to compute a printable representation of the rational number.

What values will the Rational class need to implement these responsibilities?

Lab 1: Objects

Are there any constraints on these values?

Here is a list of constructors and methods that will be used to implement the responsibilities. Fill in the missing pre-conditions, post-conditions, and test cases.

`Rational()`
> Pre-condition: none.
> Post-condition: The rational number 1 has been constructed.
> Test cases: none.

`Rational(n, d)`
> Pre-condition: The denominator d is non-zero.
> Post-condition: The rational number n/d has been constructed and is in normal form.
> Test cases:

n = 2,	d = 4;	result is 1/2
n = 0,	d = 7;	result is 0/1
n = 12,	d = –30;	result is –2/5
n = 4,	d = 0;	result is Exception

`int getNumerator()`
> Pre-condition: The rational n/d is in a valid state.
> Post-condition: The value n is returned.
> Test cases:

n/d is 1/2;	result is 1
n/d is 0/1;	result is 0
n/d is –2/5;	result is –2

`int getDenominator()`

 Pre-condition:

 Post-condition:

 Test cases:

`Rational negate()`
> Pre-condition: The rational n/d is in a valid state.
> Post-condition: The rational number –n/d has been returned.

 Test cases:

`Rational reciprocal()`

 Pre-condition:

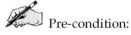 Post-condition:

 Test cases:

```
boolean equals(Object other)
```

 Pre-condition:

 Post-condition:

 Test cases:

```
Rational sum (Rational other)
```
Pre-condition: The rational n/d is in a valid state and other is the valid rational x/y.
Post-condition: The rational number (ny+xd)/dy has been returned.
Test cases:

n/d is 1/2, x/y is 1/2;	result is 1/1
n/d is 1/2, x/y is 1/6;	result is 2/3
n/d is 3/4, x/y is 5/6;	result is 19/12
n/d is 1/3, x/y is –2/3;	result is –1/3

```
Rational difference(Rational other)
```

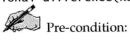 Pre-condition:

 Post-condition:

 Test cases:

```
Rational multiply(Rational other)
```

 Pre-condition:

 Post-condition:

 Test cases:

`Rational divide(Rational other)`

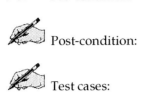 Pre-condition:

 Post-condition:

Test cases:

`String toString()`
Pre-condition: The rational n/d is in a valid state.
Post-condition: The string "n/d" has been returned.
Test cases:

n/d is 1/2;	result is "1/2"
n/d is 0/1;	result is "0/1"
n/d is –2/5;	result is "–2/5"

Counter

The counter will be a class that acts like a simple click counter (used for counting attendance) with a few improvements. The click counter will have a minimum and maximum value. It will start at the minimum value. Each click will add one to the counter, except when the counter hits the maximum value, where it will roll back over to the minimum. The click counter will also support an operation that decreases the value of the counter by one. If this would decrease the value below the minimum, it will roll over to the maximum value.

Think about the preceding description and give a list of responsibilities for the Counter class.

What values will the Counter class need to implement these responsibilities?

Are there any constraints on these values?

Give a list of constructors and methods that will be used to implement the responsibilities you have listed. Fill in the pre-conditions, post-conditions, and test cases.

Directed Lab Work

Rational

The skeleton of the Rational class already exists and is in *Rational.java*. Test code has been created and is in *RationalTest.java*. You will complete the methods for the Rational class.

Step 1. If you have not done so, look at the interface documentation in *Rational.html*. Look at the skeleton in *Rational.java*. All of the methods exist, but do not yet do anything. Compile the classes ZeroDenominatorException, Rational, and RationalTest. Run the main method in RationalTest.

Checkpoint: If all has gone well, you should see test results. Don't worry for now about whether the test cases are passes or fails. Don't worry about the null pointer exception. All we want to see is that the Rational class has the correct protocol. Now you will complete the heart of the Rational class, its constructors, and basic accessor methods.

Step 2. Create private variables that will hold the state of a Rational object.

Step 3. Complete the default constructor. It should create the rational number 1.

Step 4. Complete the private method normalize. It should put the rational number in a normal form where the numerator and denominator share no common factors. Also, guarantee that only the numerator is negative. The gcd (greatest common divisor) method may be of use to you.

Step 5. Complete the alternate constructor. It should throw a new ZeroDenominatorException if needed. Don't forget to normalize.

Step 6. Complete the method getNumerator().

Step 7. Complete the method getDenominator().

Checkpoint: At this point there is enough to test. Your code should compile and pass all the tests in testConstructor(). If it fails any tests, debug and retest. The next two methods chosen for implementation are simple methods that construct a new rational number using the object.

Step 8. Complete the method negate(). Note that this method should not change the rational number it is invoked on, but return a new object. Don't forget to change the return statement. Currently it returns null, which means after executing the line of code

```
Rational r2 = r1.negate();
```

the variable r2 will have the value null. If any methods are invoked on null (e.g., r2.getNumerator()) a null pointer exception will occur.

Checkpoint: Your code should compile and pass all the tests up to and including testNegate(). If it fails any tests, debug and retest.

Step 9. Complete the method reciprocal().

Checkpoint: Your code should compile and pass all the tests through testInvert(). If it fails any tests, debug and retest. The next two methods chosen for implementation are closely related and will be tested together.

Step 10. Complete the method add().

Step 11. Complete the method subtract(). There are a couple of ways that you can implement subtraction. One way is to use a formula similar to the one used for addition. The other way is to negate the second argument and then add. Either technique will work.

Checkpoint: Your code should compile and pass all the tests through testAddSubtract(). *If it fails any tests, debug and retest. Again the next two methods are closely related and will be implemented together.*

Step 12. Complete the method multiply().

Step 13. Complete the method divide().

Final checkpoint: Your code should compile and pass all the tests.

Counter

The skeleton of the Counter class already exists and is in *Counter.java*. Test code has been created and is in *CounterTest.java*. You will complete the methods for the Counter class.

Step 1. If you have not done so, look at the interface documentation in *Counter.html*. Look at the skeleton in *Counter.java*. All of the methods exist, but do not do anything yet. Compile the classes CounterInitializationException, Counter, and CounterTest. Run the main method in CounterTest.

Checkpoint: If all has gone well, you should see test results. Don't worry for now about whether the test cases are passes or fails. All we want to see is that the Counter class has the correct protocol. Again we will work from the heart of the class outward. Your first task is to complete the constructors.

Step 2. Create private variables that will hold the state of a Counter object.

Step 3. Complete the default constructor. It should create a counter with a minimum of 0 and a maximum that is the largest possible integer value (Integer.MAX_VALUE).

Step 4. Complete the alternate constructor. It should check to see if the minimum value is less than the maximum value and throw an exception if not.

Checkpoint: At this point we will verify that the exception is correctly generated. Your code should compile and pass all the tests in testConstructor(). *If it fails any tests, debug and retest. This is not a complete test of the constructors and you may have to revise them. The* toString() *method is useful to implement early because it reports on the state of an object without affecting it. It can then be used in later test cases. It is also one of the methods that classes typically override.*

Step 5. Complete the method toString().

Checkpoint: Your code should compile. There is no mandated format for your toString() *method. Check that it produces all the information given by the print statements in* testToString. *If not, debug and retest. Another method that is typically overridden is the* equals() *method. You will work with it next.*

Step 6. Complete the method equals(). It has been started for you and will test to make sure that the other object is of the same type. Complete the then clause of the if statement to check that all the private state variables have the same value.

Checkpoint: Your code should compile and pass all the tests through testEquals(). *If it fails any tests, debug and retest. There are two final accessor methods to complete and then the mutators will be implemented.*

Step 7.   Complete the method value().

Step 8.   Complete the method rolledOver().

Step 9.   Complete the method increase().

Check point: Your code should compile and pass all the tests through testIncrease(). If it fails any tests, debug and retest. This is really the first test that exercises a major portion of the responsibilities of the Counter class. Up until now the state of the class should not have been affected by the methods. We use the accessors to test the state of the object after the mutator has been called.

Step 10.   Complete the method decrease().

Checkpoint: Your code should compile and pass all the tests. The tests in testDecrease() are similar to what you have seen before. The decrease mutator is applied and the state is queried using the accessors. There is a different style of test being performed by testCombined(). It tests to see if the increase and decrease mutators are inverses of one another. Most of the time an increase followed by a decrease should leave the object in its original state.

Post-Lab Follow-Ups

1. Compare the test cases from the RationalTest class with the ones you created in the Pre-Lab. Were there kinds of test cases that you did not consider? Were there kinds of test cases that you proposed that were not in the RationalTest class?

2. Compare the constructors and methods from the Counter class with the methods you proposed in the Pre-Lab. Were there methods that you did not consider? Were there methods you proposed that were not in the Counter class? Do expectations for the methods as expressed in the CounterTest class differ from what you expected? Can you justify your omissions and additions?

3. Implement and test equals and toString for the Rational class.

4. Think further about a class that would represent a bank account. Give responsibilities for it. List the variables and any constraints. Give a list of methods with their pre-conditions, post-conditions, and test cases.

5. Think about a class that would represent a colored triangle that could be displayed on a computer screen. Give responsibilities for it. List the variables and any constraints. Give a list of methods with their pre-conditions, post-conditions, and test cases.

Lab 2   List Client

Goal

In this lab you will complete two applications that use the Abstract Data Type (ADT) list.

Resources

- Chapter 4: Lists
- *ListInterface.html*—Interface documentation for the interface *ListInterface*
- *java.sun.com/j2se/1.5.0/docs/api*—API documentation for the Java *List* interface

Java Files

- *ListInterface.java*
- *AList.java*
- *CountingGame.java*
- *Primes.java*

Introduction

The ADT list is one of the basic tools for use in developing software applications. It is an ordered collection of objects that can be accessed based on their position. Before continuing the lab you should review the material in Chapter 4. In particular, review the documentation of the interface *ListInterface.java*. While not all of the methods will be used in our applications, most of them will.

The first application you will complete implements a child's selection game. In the standard version of this game, a group of children gather in a circle and begin a rhyme. (One such rhyme goes "Engine, engine number nine, going down Chicago line. If the train should jump the track, will you get your money back? My mother told me to pick the very best one and you are not it.") Each word in the rhyme is chanted in turn by one person in the circle. The last person is out of the game and the rhyme is restarted from the next person. Eventually, one person is left and he or she is the lucky individual that is selected. This application will read the number of players in the game and the rhyme from the keyboard. The final output will be the number of the selected person. You will use two lists in this application. The first will be a list of numbers representing the players in the game. The second will be a list of words in the rhyme.

The second application is one that computes prime numbers.

Pre-Lab Visualization

Counting Game

Suppose we have six players named 1, 2, 3, 4, 5, and 6. And the rhyme has three words A, B, C. There will be five rounds played. Fill in the players next to the part of the rhyme they say in each round. Cross out the players as they are eliminated. As an example, the first round has been completed already.

	Round 1	Round 2	Round 3	Round 4	Round 5
A	1				
B	2				
C	3				

Eliminated Players: 1 2 ~~3~~ 4 5 6

Suppose we have five players named 1, 2, 3, 4, and 5. And the rhyme has six words A, B, C, D, E, F. There will be four rounds played. Fill in the players next to the part of the rhyme they say in each round. Cross out the players as they are eliminated.

	Round 1	Round 2	Round 3	Round 4
A				
B				
C				
D				
E				
F				

 Eliminated Players: 1 2 3 4 5

Primes

Suppose you are interested in finding the primes between 2 and 15 inclusive. The list of candidates would be as follows:

Candidates: 2 3 4 5 6 7 8 9 10 11 12 13 14 15

The algorithm proceeds in rounds. In each round a single prime is discovered.

Round 1:

Cross the first value off of the Candidates list and add it to the Primes list. Cross out any candidate that is divisible by the prime you have just discovered and add it to the composites list.

 Primes:

 *Composites:*

Round 2:

To make the operation of the algorithm clearer, copy the contents of the lists as they appear at the end of the previous round.

Cross the first value off of the Candidates list and add it to the Primes list. Cross out any candidate that is divisible by the prime you have just discovered and add it to the composites list.

Candidates:

Primes:

Composites:

Round 3:

Again, copy the contents of the lists as they appear at the end of the previous round.

Cross the first value off of the Candidates list and add it to the Primes list. Cross out any candidate that is divisible by the prime you have just discovered and add it to the composites list.

Candidates:

Primes:

Composites:

You can complete the other rounds if you wish, but most of the interesting work has been completed.

Finding Composites

The heart of this algorithm is removing the composite values from the candidates list. Let's examine this process more closely. In the first round, after removing the 2, the list of candidates is

Candidates: 3 4 5 6 7 8 9 10 11 12 13 14 15

How many values are in the list?

The first value to be examined is the 3. What is its index?

The second value to be examined is the 4. What is its index?

Since it is divisible by 2, we need to remove it from the list of candidates. What is the new list of candidates after the 4 is removed?

 Candidates:

The third value to be examined is the 5. What is its index?

The fourth value to be examined is the 6. What is its index?

Since it is divisible by 2, we need to remove it from the list of candidates. What is the new list of candidates after the 6 is removed?

 Candidates:

The fifth value to be examined is the 7. What is its index?

Can you simply loop over the indices from 1 to 13 to examine all the candidates?

Develop an algorithm to examine all the values in the candidates list and remove them if they are divisible by the given prime.

Directed Lab Work

Counting Game

Pieces of the CountingGame class already exist and are in *CountingGame.java*. Take a look at that code now if you have not done so already. Also, before you start make sure you are familiar with the methods available to you in the AList class (check *ListInterface.html*).

Step 1. Compile the classes CountingGame and AList. Run the main method in CountingGame.

Checkpoint: If all has gone well, the program will run and accept input. It will then generate a null pointer exception. The goal now is to create the list of players.

Step 2. Create a new Alist<Integer> and assign it to players.

Step 3. Using a loop, add new objects of type Integer to the players list.

Checkpoint: Compile and run the program. Enter 3 for the number of players. The program should print out
{ <1> <2> <3> } for the players list. The next goal is to do one round of the game. It will be encapsulated in the method doRhyme().

Step 4. Complete the doRhyme() method. Use the following algorithm.

> **For each word in the rhyme**
> **Print the word in the rhyme and the player that says it.**
> **Print the name of the player to be removed.**
> **Remove that player from the list.**
> **Return the index of the player that will start the next round.**

Step 5. Call doRhyme(players, rhyme, position) in main after the call to getRhyme().

Step 6. Print out the new player list.

Checkpoint: Compile and run the program. Enter 6 for the number of players. Enter A B C for the rhyme. It should print out something similar to
> *Player 1: a*
> *Player 2: b*
> *Player 3: c*
> *Removing player 3*
> *The players list is { <1> <2> <4> <5> <6> }*
Enter 5 for the number of players. Enter A B C D E F for the rhyme. Compare your result with your answers in the Pre-Lab. Reconcile any differences. The final goal is to do multiple rounds.

Step 7. Wrap the lines of code from the previous two steps in a while loop that continues as long as there is more than one player left.

Final checkpoint: Compile and run the program. Enter 6 for the number of players. Enter A B C for the rhyme. The players should be removed in the order 3, 6, 4, 2, 5. The winner should be player 1.

Enter 5 for the number of players. Enter A B C D E F for the rhyme. Compare your result with your answers in the Pre-Lab Exercises. Reconcile any differences.

Primes

The skeleton of the Primes class already exists and is in *Primes.java*.

Step 1.   Look at the skeleton in *Primes.java*. Compile Primes. Run the main method in Primes.

Checkpoint: If all has gone well, the program will run and accept input. It will then end. The goal now is to create the list of candidates.

Step 2.   In main declare and create the Candidates list. Add in the values.

Step 3.   Print out the candidates list.

Checkpoint: Compile and run the program. Enter 7 for the maximum value. You should see the list { <2> <3> <4> <5> <6> <7> }. The next goal is to do a single round finding a prime in the Candidates list.

Step 4.   In main declare and create the Primes and Composites lists.

Step 5.   Remove the first value from the primes list and store it in an Integer variable. Remember to type cast the value returned by remove().

Step 6.   Print out the prime that was discovered.

Step 7.   Add it to the primes list.

Step 8.   Print out all three lists.

Checkpoint: Compile and run the program. Enter 7 for the maximum value. The value 2 should be removed from the Candidates list and added to the Primes. Now all values that are divisible by the Prime should be removed from the Candidates list and added to the Composites list. This procedure will be encapsulated in the method getComposites().

Step 9.   Refer to the Pre-Lab Exercises and complete the getComposites() method. To determine if one integer value is divisible by another, you can use the modulus operator (% in Java).

Step 10.   Between the code from steps 7 and 8, call getComposites().

Checkpoint: Compile and run the program. Enter 15 for the maximum value. Compare the results with the Pre-Lab Exercises. Reconcile any differences.

Just as in the counting game, a loop will be used to do the rounds.

Step 11. Wrap the code from steps 5 through 8 in a `while` loop that continues as long as the Candidates list is not empty.

Final checkpoint: Compile and run the program. Enter 15 for the maximum value. Compare the results with the Pre-Lab Exercises. Reconcile any differences.

Run the program with 100 as the maximum value. Carefully verify your results.

Post-Lab Follow-Ups

1. Modify the counting game program to compute the winning player for all sizes of player lists up to the input value. Complete a table for player lists up to size 20 with a rhyme of length 3. Can you discover a relation between the size of the player list and the winning player?

2. After a certain point, all the remaining values in the candidates list are prime. Modify the program to just copy values directly when that point has been reached.

3. Write a program that will get a list of words and then remove any duplicates.

4. Write a program that will get two lists of words and will create a third list that consists of any words in common between the two input lists.

5. Write a program that will read in a list of words and will create and display two lists. The first list will be the words in odd positions of the list. The second list will be all the remaining words.

6. Write a program that will get a list of integer values and determine if all the values are relatively prime. Two values are relatively prime if they share no common factors. For example, the values 10 and 77 are relatively prime, but 10 and 55 are not.

Lab 3   Array Based List Implementation

Goal

In this lab you will explore the implementation of the ADT list using arrays. You will take an existing implementation and create new methods that work with that implementation. You will override the `equals` method so that it will determine if two lists are equal based on their contents. You will implement a `swap` method that will exchange two items in the list. You will implement a `reverse` method that will reverse the order of the items in the list. Finally, you will implement a `cycle` method that will move the first item in the list to the last position.

Resources

- Chapter 2: Creating Classes from Other Classes
- Chapter 4: Lists
- Chapter 5: List Implementations That Use Arrays
- *ListInterface.html*—Interface documentation for the interface `ListInterface`

Java Files

- *ListInterface.java*
- *AList.java*
- *ListExtensionsTest.java*

Introduction

As was seen in the last lab, a list is an ordered collection of elements supporting basic operations such as add and remove. One way to implement a list is to use an array. The other standard implementation is a linked structure (which will be investigated in the next lab). In this lab, you will take a working implementation and create some new methods. If you have not done so already, take a moment to examine the code in *AList.java*.

Consider the code that implements the add method.

```
public boolean add(int newPosition, T newEntry) {
    boolean isSuccessful = true;

    if (isArrayFull())
        doubleArray();

    if ( (newPosition >= 1) && (newPosition <= length+1)) {
      makeRoom(newPosition);
      list[newPosition-1] = newEntry;
      length++;
    }
    else
      isSuccessful = false;

    return isSuccessful;
} // end add

private void makeRoom(int newPosition) {
    assert (newPosition >= 1) && (newPosition <= length + 1);
    int newIndex = newPosition - 1;
    int lastIndex = length - 1;
    // move each entry to next higher index, starting at end of
    // array and continuing until the entry at newIndex is moved
    for (int index = lastIndex; index >= newIndex; index--)
        list[index + 1] = list[index];
} // end makeRoom
```

Let's trace the last statement in the following code fragment.

```
AList<String> x = new AList<String>(5);
x.add("a");
x.add("b");
x.add("c");
x.add("d");
x.add(2, "x");          // trace this one
```

The initial state of the object is

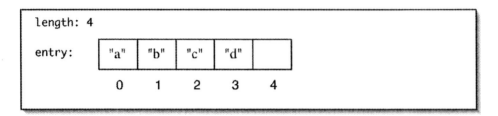

The variable isSuccessful is initialized.
The array is not full, so the condition (isArrayFull()) is false.

```
newPosition: 2
object : "x"
isSuccessful: true
```

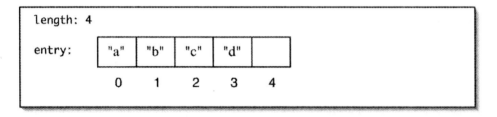

The condition ((newPosition >= 1) && (newPosition <= length+1)) is true, so makeRoom(2) is invoked. The first execution of the body of the loop results in the following state.

```
newPosition: 2
index: 4
```

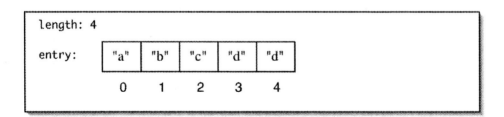

The second execution of the body of the loop results in the following state.

```
newPosition: 2
index: 3
```

```
length: 4

entry:   "a" | "b" | "c" | "c" | "d"
          0     1     2     3     4
```

The third and final execution of the body of the loop (index >= newPosition) results in the following state.

```
newPosition: 2
index: 2
```

```
length: 4

entry:   "a" | "b" | "b" | "c" | "d"
          0     1     2     3     4
```

The makeRoom() method returns and the next line puts the object into the array.

```
newPosition: 2
object : "x"
isSuccessful: true
```

```
length: 4

entry:   "a" | "x" | "b" | "c" | "d"
          0     1     2     3     4
```

The final statement before the add() method returns adjusts the length, resulting in the final state of the list.

```
length: 5

entry:   "a" | "x" | "b" | "c" | "d"
          0     1     2     3     4
```

Notice that to the client, the position of the first item in the list is 1. Internally, however, the AList implementation stores the first item at index 0 of the array.

The first thing that you will do in this lab is to override the `equals` method. Every class inherits the `equals` method from the class `Object`. The inherited method determines if two objects are equal based on their identity. Only if two objects are located at the same memory location will the `equals` method return true. Instead of this, we need to know if two lists are the same based on whether their contents are the same. The new version of `equals` will then be used to decide if the implementations of other methods you create are correct. Once the equals method has been completed correctly, the other three methods can be completed in any order.

The swap operation will be an exchange of neighbors. The general form of swapping allows you to exchange any two items and is a widely used operation in many sorting algorithms. Our version of swap will be limited to swapping neighboring items. (This will be easier to implement in the next lab which deals with a linked representation.) The swap method will take as its only argument the position of the second item to be swapped. So swap(5) will exchange the fourth and fifth items in the list. To be consistent with the other methods in the `ListInterface`, it will return a boolean value that indicates a successful swap. It will fail if the value of the second position is not valid.

One way that the `swap()` method could be implemented is shown in the following code, which uses the public methods of the `ListInterface`.

```
public boolean swap(int secondPosition)
{
    boolean result = false;
    if (secondPosition > 1
        && secondPosition <= getLength())
    {
        T x = remove(secondPosition);
        boolean removeGood = (x != null);
        boolean addGood = add(secondPosition-1, x);
        result = removeGood && addGood;
    }
    return result;
}
```

This code has the advantage of not needing to change if the implementation of the class changes. On the other hand, it may be less efficient than a method that directly accesses the private variables of the class. Since the goal of the lab is to become more familiar with the array implementation of the `AList`, you will work directly with the `entry` array and will not use methods from the interface like `add()` or `remove()`.

The cycle operation can be used in a number of different applications. One example is a list of days in the week. At the start of the week, the list is (Sunday, Monday, Tuesday, Wednesday, Thursday, Friday, Saturday). As each day passes, the list will be cycled by moving the first item to the end of the list. On Monday, for example, the list will be cycled to (Monday, Tuesday, Wednesday, Thursday, Friday, Saturday, Sunday).

Pre-Lab Visualization

Equals

One way to determine that two lists are equal is by comparing corresponding items. Consider the following two lists. Which items need to be compared to determine that they are equal?

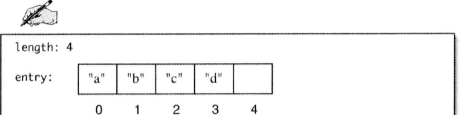

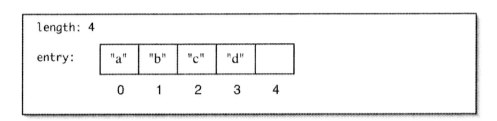

Consider the following two lists. Which items need to be compared to determine that they are not equal?

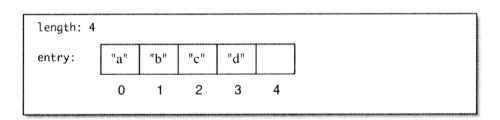

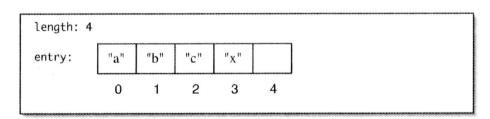

Give an example of two lists that cannot be equal, yet no item comparisons are needed to make that determination.

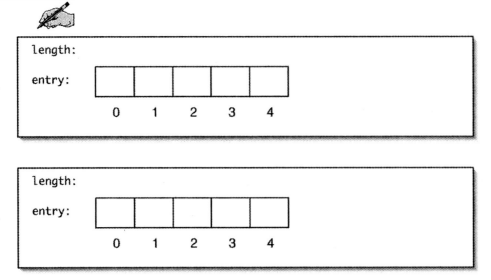

Write an algorithm that returns true if the items in two lists are pairwise `equals`.

Swap

Suppose there is a list with the following state:

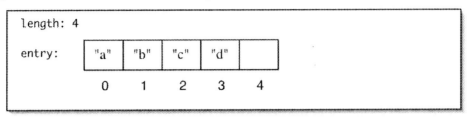

What will the final state be after swap(3)? Remember that the item in position 3 of the list has index 2.

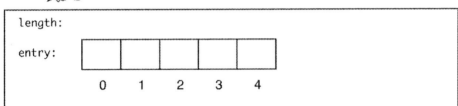

To reach the final state, follow these steps. Show the state of the list after each step.

    a. Remember the value of the second item to be swapped.

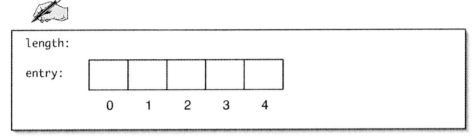

    b. Copy the first item into the position of the second item.

length:

entry:

0   1   2   3   4

c. Copy the remembered value in the position of the first item.

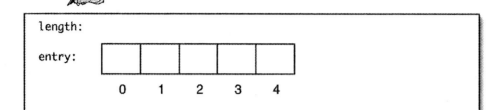

length:

entry:

```
+---+---+---+---+---+
|   |   |   |   |   |
+---+---+---+---+---+
  0   1   2   3   4
```

Write an algorithm to implement swap.

Reverse

Suppose there is a list with the following state:

length: 6

entry:

```
+-----+-----+-----+-----+-----+-----+-----+
| "a" | "b" | "c" | "d" | "e" | "f" |     |
+-----+-----+-----+-----+-----+-----+-----+
   0     1     2     3     4     5     6
```

What will the final state be after reverse()?

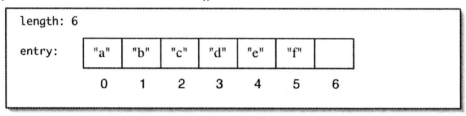

length:

entry:

```
+---+---+---+---+---+---+---+
|   |   |   |   |   |   |   |
+---+---+---+---+---+---+---+
  0   1   2   3   4   5   6
```

To reach the final state, follow these steps. Show the state of the list after each step.

a. Swap the items in the first and last positions.

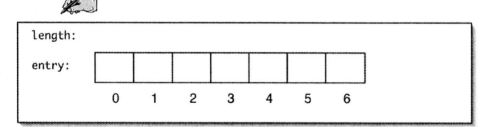

length:

entry:

```
+---+---+---+---+---+---+---+
|   |   |   |   |   |   |   |
+---+---+---+---+---+---+---+
  0   1   2   3   4   5   6
```

b. Swap the items in the second and second to last positions.

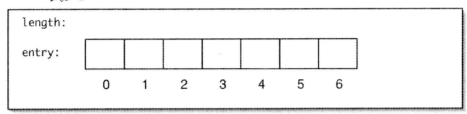

c. Swap the items in the third and third to last positions.

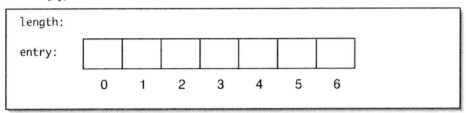

To be general, a loop will be needed.

If there are *n* items in the list, what will be the indices of the first items in the swaps?

What will be the indices of the second items in the swaps?

Write an algorithm to implement reverse.

Cycle

Suppose there is a list with the following state:

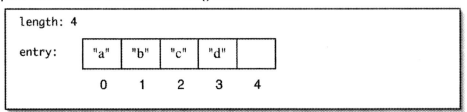

length: 4

entry:

"a"	"b"	"c"	"d"	
0	1	2	3	4

What will the final state be after `cycle()`?

length:

entry:

0	1	2	3	4

To reach the final state, follow these steps. Show the state of the list after each step.

    a.   Remember the first item.

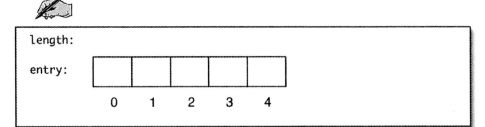

length:

entry:

0	1	2	3	4

    b.   Copy each item down one position.

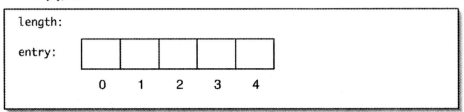

length:

entry:

0	1	2	3	4

    c.   Copy the remembered item to the last position.

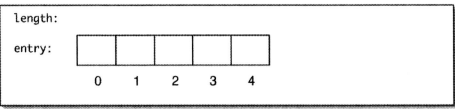

length:

entry:

0	1	2	3	4

Again, a loop will be needed.

                                                Lab 3: Array Based List Implementation

If there are *n* items in the list, what are the indices of the items that are copied?

What are the indices of the locations that the items are copied into?

Write an algorithm to implement cycle.

Directed Lab Work

The AList class is a working implementation of the *ListInterface.java*. The four methods you will be working on already exist but do not function yet. Take a look at that code now if you have not done so already.

Equals

Step 1. Compile the classes ListExtensionsTest and AList. Run the main method in ListExtensionsTest.

Checkpoint: If all has gone well, the program will run and the test cases for the four methods that will be implemented will execute. Don't worry yet about the results of the tests yet. The goal now is to finish the implementation of each of our methods one at a time.

Step 2. In the equals method of AList, implement your algorithm from the Pre-Lab Exercises. Some kind of iteration will be required in this method.

Checkpoint: Compile and run ListExtensionsTest. The tests for equals should all pass. If not, debug and retest.

Swap

Step 1. In the swap method of AList, check the argument to make sure it is good. If it is not, return false. Don't forget to change the return statement.

Checkpoint: Compile and run ListExtensionsTest. The first two tests of checkSwap should pass. If not, debug and retest.

Step 2. Complete the implementation of your algorithm from the Pre-Lab Exercises. No iteration is needed for this method. Don't forget to change the return statement.

Step 3. Before compiling, check to make sure that the code is working with the correct elements in the entry array. Remember that the item in position 3 of the list is at index 2 of the array.

Checkpoint: Compile and run ListExtensionsTest. All tests up through checkSwap should pass. If not, debug and retest.

Reverse

Step 4.   In the `reverse` method of `AList`, implement your algorithm from the Pre-Lab Exercises. Iteration is needed.

Checkpoint: Compile and run `ListExtensionsTest`. All tests up through `checkReverse` should pass. If not, debug and retest.

Cycle

Step 5.   In the `cycle` method of `AList`, implement your algorithm from the Pre-Lab Exercises. This method needs some form of iteration, but it may not be explicit. It can use the private methods of the `AList` class to avoid an explicit loop in the `cycle` method. Either way is acceptable.

Final checkpoint: Compile and run `ListExtensionsTest`. All tests should pass. If not, debug and retest.

Post-Lab Follow-Ups

1. Create test cases for the other methods in `AList`.

2. Would the `equals()` method work if one of the items in the list was `null`? Create test cases for this situation and redo the equals code if it does not pass.

3. In a list of size 10, how many assignments are made using the `entry` array if we `swap` positions 5 and 6?

4. In a list of size 10, how many assignments are made using the `entry` array by the `reverse` method?

5. In a list of size 10, how many assignments are made using the `entry` array by the `cycle` method?

6. Implement the general form of the `swap` method using direct access to the `entry` array.

    ```
    boolean swap(int first, int second){
    ...
    }
    ```

7. Implement the general `swap` method using only the public methods in `ListInterface`.

8. Implement the `reverse` method using only the public methods in `ListInterface`.

Lab 4   Link Based List Implementation

Goal

In this lab you will explore the implementation of the ADT list using a linked chain. To allow you to see the difference with the array implementation, the methods you will implement will be the same as in the previous lab (equals, swap, reverse, and cycle).

Resources

- Chapter 2: Creating Classes from Other Classes
- Chapter 4: Lists
- Chapter 6: List Implementations That Link Data
- Chapter 7: Completing the Linked Implementation of a List
- *ListInterface.html*—Interface documentation for the interface ListInterface

Java Files

- *ListInterface.java*
- *LList.java*
- *ListExtensionsTest.java*

Introduction

In the last lab, you saw an array implementation of the ADT list. In this lab, you will work with a singly linked chain. If you have not done so already, take a moment to examine the code in *LList.java*.

Consider the code that implements the add operation.

```
public boolean add(int newPosition, T newEntry)
{
    boolean isSuccessful = true;

    if ((newPosition >= 1) && (newPosition <= length+1))
    {
        Node newNode = new Node(newEntry);
        if (isEmpty() || (newPosition == 1))   // case 1
        {
            newNode.next = firstNode;
            firstNode = newNode;
        }
        else // case 2: newPosition >1, list is not empty
        {
            Node nodeBefore = getNodeAt(newPosition - 1);
            Node nodeAfter = nodeBefore.next;
            newNode.next = nodeAfter;
            nodeBefore.next = newNode;
        } // end if
        length++;
    }
    else
        isSuccessful = false;
    return isSuccessful;
} // end add
```

Let's trace the last statement in the following code fragment.

```
LList<String> x = new LList()<String>;
x.add("a");
x.add("b");
x.add("c");
x.add("d");
x.add(2, "x");        // trace this one
```

The initial state of the object is

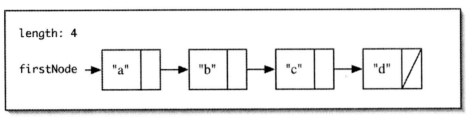

The condition ((newPosition >= 1) && (newPosition <= length+1)) is true.
A new node is created.

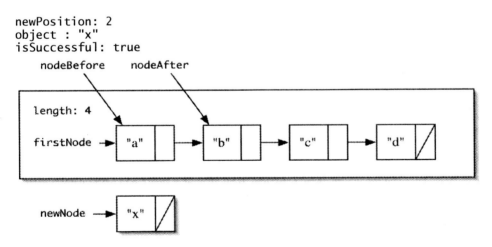

The condition (isEmpty() || (newPosition == 1)) is false since the insertion is not at the front of the list. The else branch is chosen. The local variable nodeBefore is set to getNodeAt(1). Then the variable nodeAfter is set.

newPosition: 2
object : "x"
isSuccessful: true

The next reference for the new node is set to be the node after the insertion point.

```
newPosition: 2
object : "x"
isSuccessful: true
```

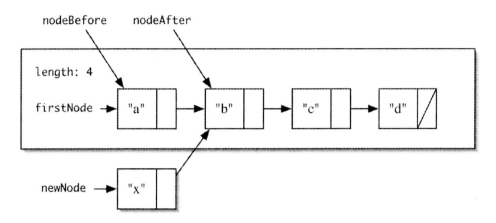

Finally, the new node is linked into the list by setting the next reference of the node before and the length is updated.

```
newPosition: 2
object : "x"
isSuccessful: true
```

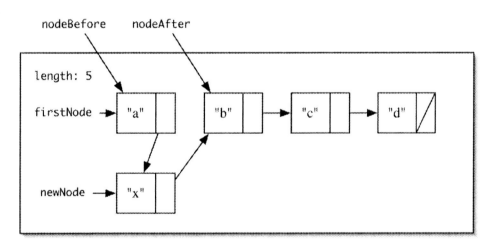

As in the last lab, the first task is to override the `equals` method. The same basic algorithm will be used as last time except that there is no direct access to the elements. Instead two references, one to each list, will be used to scan across the elements.

The other methods will all require list surgery. The values in the nodes will not be changed, only the links. Unfortunately, if you are not careful, the list will not survive the surgery. Let's see how you could get into trouble.

The change that will be made is not inherently dangerous. The variable nodeAfter is not absolutely necessary. It can be replaced by its definition in the two lines that do the list surgery.

```
newNode.next = nodeBefore.next;
nodeBefore.next = newNode;
```

Once this has been done, the order that the surgery is done becomes critical. Suppose the order of the two lines is switched.

```
nodeBefore.next = newNode;
newNode.next = nodeBefore.next;
```

Two bad things happen. The last part of the list is lost and the part of the list that isn't lost becomes circular.

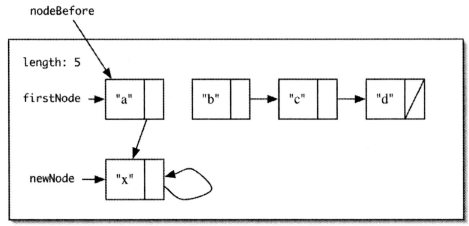

The advantage of using the variable nodeAfter is that the order of the two surgery statements does not matter.

To avoid problems with surgery, it is always a good idea to trace carefully the intended operation of methods before implementing the code.

Pre-Lab Visualization

Swap

Suppose there is a list with the following state:

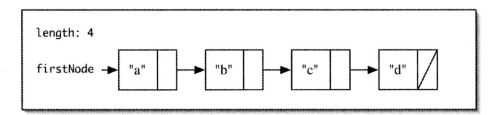

What will the final state be after swap(3)?

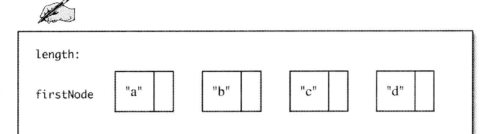

To reach the final state, follow these steps. Show the state of the list after each step.

a. Remember the position of every node in the list that had its link changed.

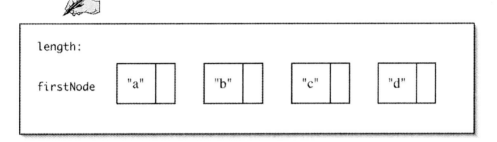

b. Change the link so that the node before the two swapped nodes now references the second node in the swap.

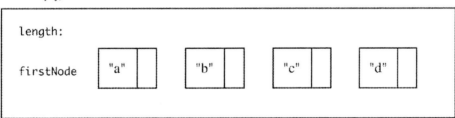

c. Change the link of the second node in the swap so that it now references the first node in the swap.

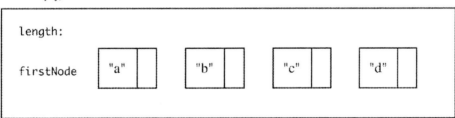

d. Change the link of the first node in the swap so that it now reference the node after the two swapped nodes.

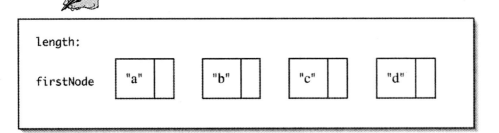

Suppose there is a list with the following state:

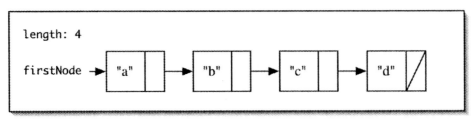

What will the final state be after `swap(2)`?

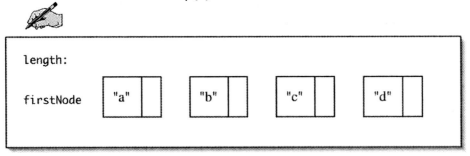

This is a special case that you need to take care of. The difference between the two examples is that one involves change a to `firstNode` and the other does not. The steps used are similar.

Write an algorithm for the general case of the swap operation (the first item in the list is not one of the pair of items to be swapped).

What changes need to be made to the general algorithm to handle the special case where the first item in the list is one of the pair of items to be swapped?

Reverse

The algorithm that will be used to reverse the linked chain is very different from that used with the array implementation. No swaps will be done, but instead the links will be altered in a single pass over the list.

Suppose there is a list with the following state:

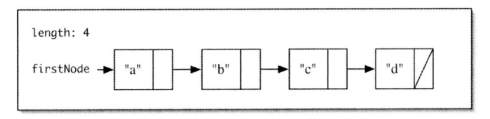

What will the final state be after reverse()?

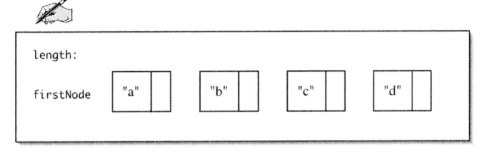

To reach the final state, follow these steps. Show the state of the list after each step.

    a. Use three variables to reference the first three nodes in the list.

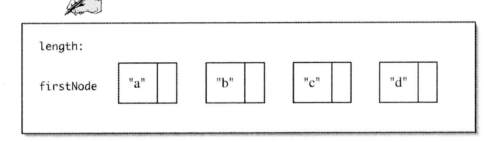

    b. Make the first node's next reference be null.

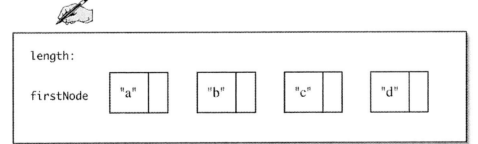

c. Make the second node's next reference be the first node. Change all three reference variables so that they move forward by one with respect to the original list.

length:

firstNode   "a" | | "b" | | "c" | | "d" | |

d. Make the third node's next reference be the second node. Change all three reference variables so that they move forward by one with respect to the original list.

length:

firstNode   "a" | | "b" | | "c" | | "d" | |

e. Make the fourth node's next reference be the third node.

length:

firstNode   "a" | | "b" | | "c" | | "d" | |

f. Change the variable firstNode so that it references the fourth node.

length:

firstNode   "a" | | "b" | | "c" | | "d" | |

To be general, a loop will be needed. Write an algorithm for the reverse operation.

Consider each of the following cases and decide if the algorithm handles it correctly.

    i.   A list with no elements
    ii.   A list with one element
    iii.   A list with two elements

Cycle

Suppose there is a list with the following state:

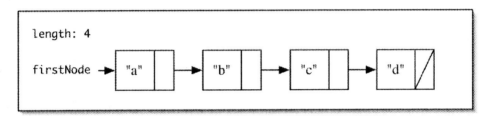

What will the final state be after cycle()?

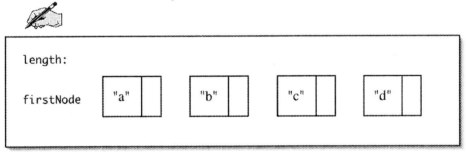

To reach the final state, follow these steps. Show the state of the list after each step.

a. Remember the position of the second node in the list. Find and remember the position of the last node in the list.

length:

firstNode |"a"| | |"b"| | |"c"| | |"d"| |

b. Make the last node's next reference be the first node.

length:

firstNode |"a"| | |"b"| | |"c"| | |"d"| |

c. Change the variable firstNode so that it references the second node.

length:

firstNode |"a"| | |"b"| | |"c"| | |"d"| |

d. Make the former first node's next reference be null.

length:

firstNode |"a"| | |"b"| | |"c"| | |"d"| |

Write an algorithm for the cycle operation.

Consider each of the following cases and decide if the algorithm handles it correctly.

   i.   A list with no elements.
   ii.   A list with one element.
   iii.   A list with two elements.

Directed Lab Work

The LList class is a working implementation of the *ListInterface.java*. The four methods you will be working on already exist but do not function yet. Take a look at that code now if you have not done so already.

Equals

Step 1. Compile the classes ExtensionsTest and LList. Run the main method in ExtensionsTest.

Checkpoint: If all has gone well, the program and the test cases will run for the four methods that will be implemented. The goal now is to finish the implementation of each of our methods one at a time.

Step 2. In the equals method of LList, implement your algorithm from the Pre-Lab Exercises. Don't forget that you will need two references, one for each list. As the iteration progresses, both references will move in synch.

Checkpoint: Compile and run ListExtensionsTest. The tests for equals should all pass. If not, debug and retest. We will implement the swap in two parts. First the general case will be completed.

Swap

Step 1. In the swap method of LList, check the argument to make sure it is good. If it is not, return false. Don't forget to change the return statement.

Checkpoint: Compile and run ListExtensionsTest. The first two tests of checkSwap should pass. If not, debug and retest.

Step 2. Now implement just your general algorithm from the Pre-Lab Exercises. Iteration will be needed in this method to find the nodes to be swapped.

Checkpoint: Compile and run ListExtensionsTest. The first five tests of checkSwap should pass. If not, debug and retest.

Step 3.   Now add in code to test for and implement the special case.

Checkpoint: Compile and run ListExtensionsTest. All tests up through checkSwap should pass. If not, debug and retest.

Reverse

Step 4.   In the reverse method of LList, implement your algorithm from the Pre-Lab Exercises. Iteration is needed.

Checkpoint: Compile and run ListExtensionsTest. All tests up through checkReverse should pass. If not, debug and retest.

Cycle

Step 5.   In the cycle method of LList, implement your algorithm from the Pre-Lab Exercises.

Final checkpoint: Compile and run ListExtensionsTest. All tests should pass. If not, debug and retest.

Post-Lab Follow-Ups

1. In a list of size 10, how many times is a next reference accessed or changed if we swap positions 5 and 6? Compare this with the answer to the Post-Lab question from the previous lab.

2. In a list of size 10, how many times is a next Post-Lab question accessed or changed by the reverse method? Compare this with the results from the previous lab.

3. In a list of size 10, how many times is a next reference accessed or changed by the cycle method? Compare this with the results from the previous lab.

4. Implement the general form of the swap method using manipulation of the next references.

    ```
    boolean swap(int first, int second)
    {
    ...
    }
    ```

5. Consider an implementation where a node has references both to the previous and next nodes. Sketch out the operations needed to implement the method.

    ```
    public boolean add(int newPosition, Object newEntry)
    ```

6. Consider an implementation where a node has references both to the previous and next nodes. Sketch out the operations needed to implement the method.

    ```
    public boolean swap(int secondPosition)
    ```

7. Implement the LList class using nodes with next and previous references. Use the test cases from the previous lab's follow-up questions if you did them. If not, create test cases and test your code.

Lab 5   Iterators

Goal

In this lab you will implement three client applications that use lists with iterators.

Resources

- Chapter 4: Lists
- Chapter 5: List Implementations That Use Arrays
- Chapter 8: Iterators
- *ListInterface.html*—documentation for the interface ListInterface
- *ListWithListIteratorInterface.html*—documentation for the interface ListWithListIteratorInterface
- *java.sun.com/j2se/1.5.0/docs/api*—API documentation for the Java Iterator interface
- *java.sun.com/j2se/1.5.0/docs/api*—API documentation for the Java ListIterator interface

Java Files

- *ListInterface.java*
- *ListWithListIteratorInterface.java*
- *ArrayListWithListIterator.java*
- *CountingGame.java*
- *Primes.java*
- *Subsequence.java*

Introduction

An iterator is an object that allows you to access the items stored in a data structure sequentially. This has two major advantages. The first advantage is that because many very different kinds of data structures have iterators defined for them, code can be written that will work independent of the choice of data structure. That code is protected against changes in data structure. For example, using Java's ListIterator, here is code that will remove all items from a data structure holding items of type X.

```
ListIterator<X> toClear = someDataStructure.getIterator();
while(toClear.hasNext())
{
    toClear.next();
    toClear.remove();
}
```

As long as the object someDataStructure has implemented the method getIterator(), the rest of the code is insulated from change. Since sequential access to a collection of items is very common, iterators are fairly useful.

The second advantage is that the iterator may be specialized to provide fast sequential access to the items in the collection. For example, consider a list that uses a linked chain. The items in a simple singly-linked chain could be accessed one at a time using a get-entry method. The only problem with this is that each time a get-entry executes, the chain must be traversed from the front. An iterator would be able to keep a reference to the nodes in the linked chain and would not have to restart from the beginning for each access.

In this lab, you will implement the counting game and primes applications from Lab 2 using iterators. You will be develop a third application that, given two sequences of objects, will determine if the first is a subsequence of the second. Before discussing what a subsequence is, consider the following formal definition.

Given X = < x_1, x_2, ..., x_n> a sequence of length n greater than or equal to zero and Y = < y_1, y_2, ..., y_m> a sequence of length m greater than or equal to zero, the function subsequence(X, Y) is true if and only if there exists a strictly increasing sequence of indices K = < k_1, k_2, ..., k_n > such that every element x_i is equal to y_j where j = k_i.

Consider the following sequences.

X = < a b a > and Y = < b c a c b a>

X is a subsequence of Y because you can find a sequence of indices that satisfies the requirements.

K = < 3 5 6>
x_1 = a is equal to y_3 = a
x_2 = b is equal to y_5 = b
x_3 = a is equal to y_6 = a

Notice that items in X must in the same order in Y but need not be consecutive. Also, because the indices in K must be strictly increasing, we cannot reuse a value in Y. Here are some examples of pairs that are not subsequences.

X = < a b a a> and Y = < b c a c b a>
X = < a b a > and Y = < b c a c b >
X = < a b c> and Y = < b c a c b a>

Many students are surprised to learn that the following pair is a subsequence.

X = < > and Y = < b c a c b a>

In this, case X is a subsequence of Y because you can find a sequence of indices, K = < >, that satisfies the requirements. Notice that every element in X is equal to an element of Y trivially. If this were not the case, you would be able to demonstrate an element from X that is not equal to the selected element of Y.

Pre-Lab Visualization

Subsequence

Come up with an example of two sequences X and Y where you can guarantee that X is not a subsequence of Y without having to look at the values of the items in the sequences.

Consider the sequences

```
X = < a  b  c  a >
Y = < b  c  d  a  e  c  a  e  a  f  b  a  b  b  d  e  c  d  e  a  b  d >
```

Match 1:

The first "a" in X must be matched with an "a" in Y.

Can it be safely matched with the first "a" in Y? (Safe in the sense that it does not prevent us from matching a later item from X.)

Can any items before the first "a" in Y be matched with an item from X?

What positions in Y must be checked to find the "a" ?

Cross out the items from both lists that have been checked to make the first match.

```
X = < a  b  c  a >
Y = < b  c  d  a  e  c  a  e  a  f  b  a  b  b  d  e  c  d  e  a  b  d >
```

Match 2:

The "b" in X must be matched with a "b" in Y.

What positions in Y must be checked to find the "b"?

Cross out the items from both lists that have been checked to make the first and second matches.

```
X = < a  b  c  a >
Y = < b  c  d  a  e  c  a  e  a  f  b  a  b  b  d  e  c  d  e  a  b  d >
```

Match 3:

The "c" in X must be matched with a "c" in Y.

What positions in Y must be checked to find the "c"?

Cross out the items from both lists that have been checked to make the first three matches.

X = < a b c a >

Y = < b c d a e c a e a f b a b b d e c d e a b d >

Match 4:

The second "a" in X must be matched with an "a" in Y.

What positions in Y must be checked to find the "a"?

Cross out the items from both lists that have been checked to make the first four matches.

X = < a b c a >

Y = < b c d a e c a e a f b a b b d e c d e a b d >

An iterator is appropriate if you checked the values sequentially. Did you check the values in both X and Y sequentially?

Develop an algorithm to detect a subsequence that uses two iterators (one `Iterator` for each sequence). It may be helpful to first develop an algorithm that works with two arrays. Looking at a value in the array, corresponds to doing a `next()`. Limit tests on the indices correspond with `hasNext()`.

Does the algorithm work if:

    i.   X is an empty sequence
    ii.   X is a sequence of length one
    iii.   Y is an empty sequence
    iv.   Y is a sequence of length one.

Counting Game

Write an algorithm for displaying all the items in a list using an `Iterator`.

One of the tasks needed in the counting game is to fill the player's list. Show how you can use an iterator to add all of the players.

Look at the code from Lab 2 for `doRhyme()`. It will be modified to use iterators. There are some major changes to the signature of `doRhyme()`. Instead of taking two lists as parameters, it will take two iterators. The integer parameter `startAt` is no longer needed, as the iterator to the player list will specify the location. No return value is needed either, since the state of the player list iterator will change.

Give an algorithm that accomplishes the same task using two list iterators (one for each list). Notice that the rhyme will start at the current entry in the player list. (You can use the `previous()` method from `ListIterator` to go backwards in the list when it is time to go back to the beginning of the list.)

Finding Composites

Look at the code from Lab 2 for getComposites(). It will be modified to use an iterator. Since getComposites always starts at the beginning of the list, it will take the list as a parameter and get its own iterator. If the iterator is passed in from the outside, getComposites would have to rely on that code to initialize the iterator correctly, and this is dangerous.

Give an algorithm using an iterator.

Directed Lab Work

Subsequence

Pieces of the Subsequence class already exist and are in *Subsequence.java*. Take a look at that code now if you have not done so already.

Step 1. Compile the class Subsequence. Run the main method in Subsequence.

Checkpoint: If all has gone well, the program will run and accept two lines of words for input. It will fail most test cases.

Step 2. Refer to your algorithm from the Pre-Lab Exercises and complete the subSequence() method.

Final checkpoint: Compile and run the program. All tests should pass. If not, debug the code so that it works correctly.

Counting Game

Pieces of the CountingGame class already exist and are in *CountingGame.java*. Take a look at that code now if you have not done so already.

Step 1. Compile the class CountingGame. Run the main method in CountingGame.

Checkpoint: If all has gone well, the program will run and accept input. It will then declare null the winner. The goal now is to create the list of players.

Step 2. Use the add() method to add the first player to the list.

Step 3. Refer to the Pre-Lab Exercises and use a loop with an iterator to add the rest of the players to the list.

Checkpoint: Compile and run the program. The program should accept input and then declare that player 1 is the winner. The next goal is to complete code that will allow collections to be displayed given an iterator.

Step 4. Compete the `displayCollection()` method. Refer to the Pre-Lab Exercises and use a loop with the iterator that is passed into the method. The desired format is opening and closing braces with spaces separating all the items. Use `print()` instead of `println()` so it will all be on the same line.

Checkpoint: Compile and run the program. The program should accept input, print the player list, and then declare that player 1 is the winner. The next goal is to do one round of the game. As before, it is encapsulated in the method doRhyme().

Step 5. Complete the `doRhyme()` method. Refer to your algorithm from the Pre-Lab Exercises.

Checkpoint: Compile and run the program. Enter 6 for the number of players. Enter A B C for the rhyme. It should print out something similar to

> *Player 1: a*
> *Player 2: b*
> *Player 3: c*
> *Removing player 3*
> *The players list is { 1 2 4 5 6 }*

Enter 5 for the number of players. Enter A B C D E F for the rhyme. Compare your result with your answers in the Pre-Lab Exercises from Lab 2. Reconcile any differences.

Step 6. Remove the `//` from the `while` loop in `main`.

Final checkpoint: Compile and run the program. Enter 6 for the number of players. Enter A B C for the rhyme. The players should be removed in the order 3, 6, 4, 2, 5. The winner should be player 1.

Enter 5 for the number of players. Enter A B C D E F for the rhyme. Compare your result with your answers in the Pre-Lab Exercises from Lab 2. Reconcile any differences.

Primes

The skeleton of the `Primes` class already exists and is in *Primes.java*.

Step 1. Look at the skeleton in *Primes.java*. Compile Primes. Run the `main` method in `Primes`.

Checkpoint: If all has gone well, the program will run and accept input. It will create the list of candidate values and display them before quitting.

Step 2. Use an iterator to print out the values in the `candidates` list at the indicated location in `main`.

Step 3. Use an iterator to print out the values in the `primes` list at the indicated location in `main`.

Step 4. Use an iterator to print out the values in the `composites` list at the indicated location in `main`.

Checkpoint: Compile and run the program. Enter 7 for the maximum value. You should see 2 3 4 5 6 7 for the candidates, 2 for the primes, and nothing for the composites. The next goal is to complete the process of removing the composite values from the candidates list. As before, it will be encapsulated in the getComposites() method.

Step 5. Refer to the Pre-Lab Exercises and complete the `getComposites()` method.

Checkpoint: Compile and run the program. Enter 15 for the maximum value. Compare the results with the Pre-Lab Exercises from Lab 2. Reconcile any differences

Step 6. Remove the `//` from the `while` loop in `main`.

Final checkpoint: Compile and run the program. Enter 15 for the maximum value. Compare the results with Pre-Lab Exercise from Lab 2. Reconcile any differences.

Run the program with 100 as the maximum value. Carefully verify your results.

Post-Lab Follow-Ups

1. Write a program using iterators that finds the longest strictly increasing subsequence in a sequence of integer values.

2. A `Set` is a collection of values that does not include duplicates and order does not matter. It will have the following methods:

   - `toString()`
   - `equals( Object )`
   - `subset( Set )`
   - `isMember( Object )`
   - `add( Object )`
   - `remove( Object )`

   Write test cases for each of the methods. **Note:** A is a subset of B if every item in A is also in B. A equals B if they agree on membership for all values. For example, { a b } equals { b a } is a subset of { c b a }. If x is added to a set A, and x is already a member of A, A does not change.

   Implement `Set` using the `ArrayListWithListIterator` class. Each of the methods (with the possible exception of `add`) should be implemented using iterators.

3. A `Bag` is a collection of values that may include duplicates. As with a set, order does not matter. It will have the following methods:

   - `toString()`
   - `equals( Object )`
   - `subbag( Bag )`
   - `isMember( Object )`
   - `count( Object )`
   - `add( Object )`
   - `remove( Object )`

   Write test cases for each of the methods. **Note:** A is a subbag of B if the count of every value x in A is less than the count of x in B. Two bags are equal if the count of every value x is the same for both bags. For example, { a b b } equals { b a b } is a subbag of { c b a b b }. Adding x to a bag will increase x's count by 1. Removing x will decrease its count by 1.

   Implement `Bag` using the `ArrayListWithListIterator` class. Each of the methods (with the possible exception of `add`) should be implemented using iterators.

4. Change `getRhyme` in `CountingGame` so that it uses an iterator to construct the list.

5. Modify `Primes` so that is uses the built-in Java class `ArrayList`. Refer to the Java API documentation.

Lab 6   Recursion—Part I

Goal

In this lab you will design and implement recursive algorithms. The primary focus in this lab will be algorithms that make a single recursive call. Tail recursion will be explored. An improved recursive algorithm for computing Fibonacci numbers will be developed.

Resources

- Chapter 10: Recursion
- *Lab6Graphs.pdf*—Printable versions of the graphs for this lab

Java Files

- *Count.java*
- *RecursiveFactorial.java*
- *TestFactorial.java*
- *RecursiveStringReplace.java*
- *TestReplace.java*
- *RecursiveFibonacci.java*
- *TestFibonacci.java*
- *TimeFibonacci.java*

Warning: The introduction and Pre-Lab materials for this lab are lengthy. Make sure to start early to give yourself enough time to complete them before the lab.

Introduction

Recursion is an important technique that shows up in diverse areas of computer science, such as the definition of computer languages, the semantics of programs, the analysis of algorithms, data structure definitions, and algorithms. Some of the better algorithms are either recursive or based on recursive algorithms. Also, recursive algorithms are often very elegant and show an economy of expression.

Since some students struggle with recursion, this lab starts out with some simple applications to improve your familiarity. The improved version of Fibonacci is a more complicated example that shows the true power of recursion. Applying yourself to this lab and the one after should get you comfortable with recursion. This will be especially useful when merge sort and quick sort are discussed and then again later when trees are presented. For students who want even more practice with recursion and functional programming, try the language Lisp. It is one of the oldest computer languages and is still in use. Its original core was strictly recursive, though iterative constructs were quickly added. Programming in Lisp or Scheme (one of its derivatives) is an interesting way to practice recursive programming.

Recursion is closely related to iteration. With the appropriate data structures, any iterative algorithm can easily be turned into a recursive algorithm. Similarly, any recursive algorithm can be made iterative. Tail recursive algorithms can be easily converted into an iterative algorithm. (Good Lisp compilers will convert tail recursive code into a loop.) Other recursive algorithms can be converted into an iterative algorithm by using a stack. (See Lab 13 for an example.) In some cases, finding an equivalent nonrecursive algorithm that does not use a stack can be quite challenging.

The basic idea of recursion is to solve a problem by first solving one or more smaller problems. Once this has been done, the solutions of the smaller problems are combined to form the solution to the original problem. The repetitive nature of recursion comes into play in that to solve the smaller problems, you first solve even smaller problems. You cannot defer the solution indefinitely. Eventually, some very small problem must be solved directly.

Recursive Design

There are five parts to designing a recursive algorithm.

Identify the problem: What are the name and arguments of the original problem to be solved?

Identify the smaller problems: What are the smaller problems that will be used to solve the original problem?

Identify how the answers are composed: Once the solutions to the smaller problems are in hand, how are they combined to get the answer to the original problem?

Identify the base cases: What are the smallest problems that must be solved directly? What are their solutions?

Compose the recursive definition: Combine the parts into a complete definition.

A recursive design for computing factorial will be used to illustrate the process. The standard recursive definition of factorial is well known (see the Resources), so a formulation will be proposed that will reduce the number of recursive calls made.

Identify the problem:
Factorial(n)

Identify the smaller problems:
(Reduce the problem size by two instead of one.)
Factorial(n – 2)

Identify how the answers are composed:
Factorial(n) = n * (n –1) * Factorial(n – 2)

Identify the base cases:
Certainly Factorial(1) is 1. But is this enough? Consider Factorial(6). Applying the recursion gives

Factorial(6) = 6*5* Factorial(4)
Factorial(6) = 6*5*4*3* Factorial(2)
Factorial(6) = 6*5*4*3*2*1* Factorial(0)
Factorial(6) = 6*5*4*3*2*1*0*(–1) Factorial(–2)
Factorial(6) = 6*5*4*3*2*1*0*(–1) *(–2) *(–3) Factorial(–4)

...

Clearly, this recursion has two chains of problems, odds and evens.

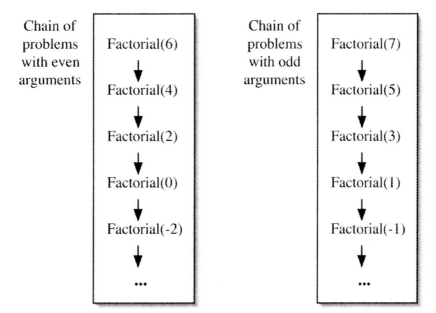

Both chains must have a base case. An appropriate question is "Where in the even chain should the recursion stop?" Looking at the last two expansions in the recursion, you see that the resulting product will be zero, which is not the correct result. No negative n is suitable for the base case. This just leaves the question of whether the base case should be Factorial(2) or Factorial(0). If Factorial(0) is the base case, what is its value? The value that makes the recursive definition work is 1.

Factorial(0) = 1
Factorial(1) = 1

Compose the recursive definition:

Factorial(n) =   1   if n=0 or n=1
                  n * (n–1) * Factorial(n–2)   if n > 1

From here you can write down the code:

```
int factorial(int n)
{
    int result;
    if( n < 2)
        result = 1;
    else
        result = n *(n-1)*factorial(n-2);
    return result;
}
```

An alternate version can be created by recognizing that the base case is simple and can be folded into the initialization.

```
int factorial(int n)
{
    int result = 1;
    if( n >= 2)
    result = n *(n-1)*factorial(n-2);
    return result;
}
```

Recursion with Structures

Consider the problem of reversing a list (or array) of values.

Identify the problem:

    Reverse(L)

Identify the smaller problems:

To reduce the size of the problem, some function of the arguments must decrease. In this case, the list L must be reduced in size. Consider the following instance of reverse:

    Reverse({ 1 2 3 4 5 }) = { 5 4 3 2 1 }

One possibility is to reduce the problem by removing the first element.

    Reverse({ 2 3 4 5 }) = { 5 4 3 2 }

This can clearly be used to get the solution to the original problem. The method tail is defined to return a list with the first element removed. (In Lisp, the tail method was originally named cdr.)

    Reverse(tail(L))

Identify how the answers are composed:

From the example, it is clear that the first element in L must be pasted onto the end of solution to the smaller problem. The method head is defined to return the first element in a list. (In Lisp, the head method was originally named car.)

Reverse(L) = append(Reverse(tail(L)), head(L))

Identify the base cases:

An empty list is the smallest possible list. It will be represented by nil. Reversing an empty list results in an empty list.

    Reverse(nil) = nil

Compose the recursive definition:

    Reverse(L) =   nil   if L is nil

                         append(Reverse(tail(L)), head(L))   if L is not nil

Code is but a short step away.

```
<T> List<T> reverse(List<T> ls)
{
    List<T> result = new ArrayList<T>();
    if( ls.size() > 0)
    {
        result =reverse( ls.subList(1,ls.size() ));
        result.add(ls.get(0));
    }
    return result;
}
```

The recursive definition used the operations append, head, and tail. In the code, the type of the argument is the built-in List class from Java. The implementation must use appropriate methods from List to accomplish the three operations. Since only a single character is being appended, the add() method can be used to place it at the end of the list. Since the first item is in location 0 of the list, get(0) will extract the head of the list. The subList() method allows one to get a range of items from the list. By starting at 1, everything except the head will be in the sublist.

There is one more thing to note about this implementation. It is functional in the sense that its argument remains unchanged. It returns a new list, which is the reverse of the argument. While this works well for the abstract definition of a list, how about an array? Each of the operations (append, head, and tail) can be implemented, but they will not be very efficient. Often for an array, it is desired that the array be changed in place.

The following redesign of the problem has the constraint that the list is stored in an array and it is desired that the reverse be done in place.

Identify the problem:
Reverse(A)
Looking ahead, there is a problem. The arguments must decrease in some fashion, yet the array will remain a constant size. What is decreasing is not the array, but the portion of the array that the recursion is working on. An auxiliary method that does the actual recursion is required.
ReverseAux(A, start, end)

Identify the smaller problems:
The portion of the array that is considered must be reduced in size. Consider the following instance of reverse:

Initially A is [1 2 3 4 5].
After ReverseAux ([1 2 3 4 5], 0, 4), A is [5 4 3 2 1].

As opposed to Reverse, ReverseAux does not return anything but has a side effect.

Suppose the same reduction in problem size is used as before (reverse the tail of the list).

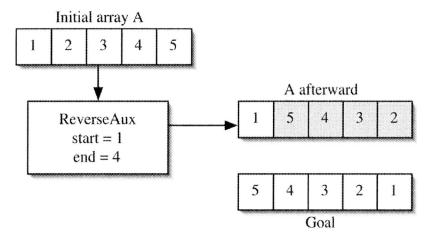

How can you get from { 1 5 4 3 2 } to { 5 4 3 2 1 }? While it is possible, it requires that every data value be moved. Trying to use ReverseAux ({ 1 2 3 4 5 }, 0, 3) results in the same kind of difficulty.

The solution is to reduce the portion of the array being worked on by moving both ends inward.

ReverseAux(A, start+1, end–1)

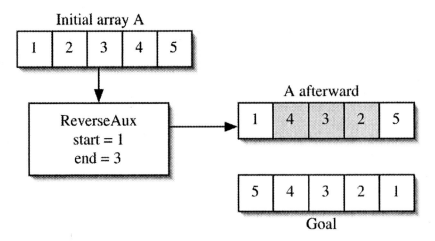

To get the desired result, all that remains is to swap the first and last elements.

Identify how the answers are composed:

ReverseAux(A, start, end) is

       1. ReverseAux(A, start+1, end–1)
       2. swap(A[start], A[end]);

Identify the base cases:

Since the reduction is by two, we have two chains of recursive method calls, one each for arrays with odd and even numbers of values to be reversed. If start is the same as end there is one value to be reversed in place. If start is less than end there is more than one value to be reversed. What if start is greater than end? It is convenient to let this represent the situation where there are no values to be reversed.

If the portion of array to be reversed is empty or contains a single element, the reverse is the same as the original and nothing needs to be done.

ReverseAux(A, x, y)   where x >= y
   is
       1. Do nothing.

Compose the recursive definition:

Reverse(A) =   ReverseAux(A, 0, A.length)

ReverseAux(A, start, end) is

       1. Do Nothing.   if start >= end
  or
       1. ReverseAux(A, start+1, end–1)   if start < end
       2. swap(A[start], A[end])

Tail Recursion

The composition work that a recursive algorithm does can either be performed before or after the recursive call. Here is a trace of the calls that ReverseAux does on a list with six elements.

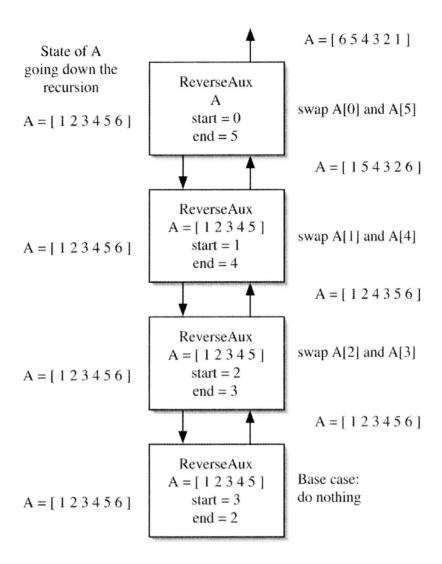

In this case the swap is done after the recursive call and all the work is done on the way back up the chain.

In a tail recursion, all the work is done on the way down the chain. Suppose that the definition is modified to become

Reverse(A) = ReverseAuxTail(A, 0, A.length)

ReverseAuxTail (A, start, end) is

1. Do Nothing.   if start >= end

or

1. swap(A[start], A[end])   if start < end
2. ReverseAuxTail (A, start+1, end–1)

Here is a trace of the calls that ReverseAuxTail does on a list with six elements.

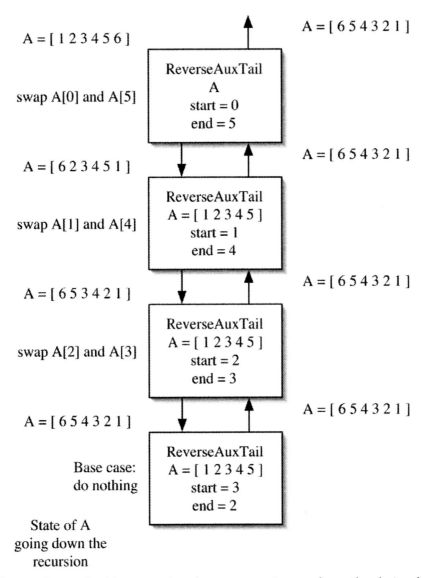

The tail recursive method is composing the answer as it goes down the chain of recursive calls. Once it reaches the base case, all the work has been done and it can return immediately. Also notice that once the next method in the chain of recursive calls is invoked, the variables start and end are no longer needed. This means that you can use an iteration that just has one copy of start and end.

In the version that is not tail recursive, start and end cannot be discarded until after the swap. Therefore, it must have multiple pairs of start and end, one for each recursive call. These will be stored on the system stack.

Often a tail recursive method will have an argument whose purpose is to store a partial solution as it is being composed. This can be illustrated by revisiting reverse on a list. Remember that the composition step was

Reverse(L) = append(Reverse(tail(L)), head(L))

In this case, the tail operation will be performed on the way down the chain of recursive calls, but the append is done on the way back up. Unlike reverse with an array, it is not simply a matter of moving statements around. The solution is to add another variable, which will hold the partial solution.

Identify the problem:
Reverse(L)

ReverseAuxTail(L, partial)

Identify the smaller problems:
Again, the size of the list will be reduced by using the tail operation. Consider the following instance of reverse:

ReverseAuxTail ({ 1 2 3 4 5 }, $partial_0$) = { 5 4 3 2 1 }

It is not clear what partial is yet, but the next call will be

ReverseAuxTail ({ 2 3 4 5 }, $partial_1$) = { 5 4 3 2 1}

Remember that the result of the final recursive call will be the final solution, so all tail recursive calls will return the solution. Continuing on,

ReverseAuxTail ({ 3 4 5 }, $partial_2$) = { 5 4 3 2 1}
ReverseAuxTail ({ 4 5 }, $partial_3$) = { 5 4 3 2 1}
ReverseAuxTail ({ 5 }, $partial_4$) = { 5 4 3 2 1}
ReverseAuxTail ({ }, $partial_5$) = { 5 4 3 2 1}

Each element must be added to the partial solution. Looking at the second to last call, the value 5 must be prepended to the front of the partial solution. (In Lisp, the prepend method is named cons.) The smaller problem is therefore:

ReverseAuxTail (tail(L), prepend(head(L), partial))

Identify how the answers are composed:
In a tail recursion, all the work in determining how to compose the final solution from the smaller problem is done in identifying the smaller problem.

ReverseAuxTail (L, partial) =
    ReverseAuxTail (tail(L), prepend(head(L), partial))

Identify the base cases:
An empty list is still the smallest possible list. It will be represented by nil. In this case, though nil is not returned. At the base case the entire solution must be ready to be returned. In fact, at this point the partial solution is complete.

ReverseAuxTail (nil, partial) = partial

Compose the recursive definition:
There is one remaining piece of business. What should the initial partial solution be? Since each of the values will be prepended to it one by one, the only possible choice is nil (an empty list).

  Reverse(L) = ReverseAuxTail (L, nil)

  ReverseAuxTail (L, partial) =

    partial   if L is nil
    ReverseAuxTail (tail(L), prepend(head(L), partial)) if L is not nil

Here is the code.

```
<T> List<T> reverse(List<T> ls)
{
    return reverseAuxTail(ls, new ArrayList<T>());
}

<T> List<T> reverseAuxTail(List<T> ls, List<T> partial)
{
    if ( ls.size() == 0)
        return partial;
    else
    {
        partial.add(0, ls.get(0));
        return reverseAuxTail(ls.subList(1,ls.size()), partial);
    }
}
```

The diagram on the next page shows a trace of the method.

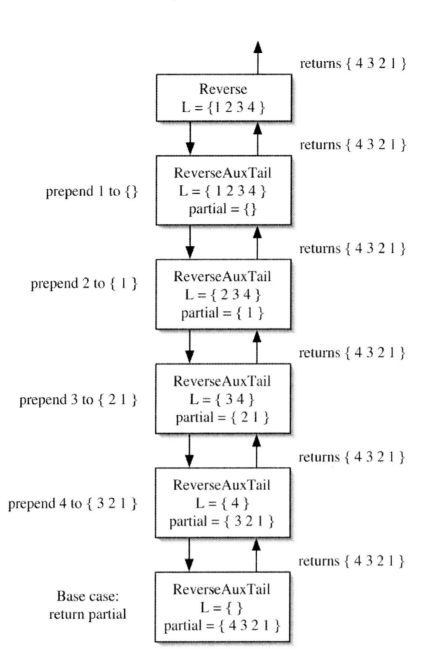

returns { 4 3 2 1 }

Reverse
L = {1 2 3 4 }

returns { 4 3 2 1 }

prepend 1 to {}

ReverseAuxTail
L = { 1 2 3 4 }
partial = {}

returns { 4 3 2 1 }

prepend 2 to { 1 }

ReverseAuxTail
L = { 2 3 4 }
partial = { 1 }

returns { 4 3 2 1 }

prepend 3 to { 2 1 }

ReverseAuxTail
L = { 3 4 }
partial = { 2 1 }

returns { 4 3 2 1 }

prepend 4 to { 3 2 1 }

ReverseAuxTail
L = { 4 }
partial = { 3 2 1 }

returns { 4 3 2 1 }

Base case:
return partial

ReverseAuxTail
L = { }
partial = { 4 3 2 1 }

Double Recursion

All of the recursive algorithms presented so far have a chain of recursive calls. Each recursive call in turn makes a single invocation of a smaller recursive problem. A number of recursive algorithms can make two or more recursive invocations. The classic example of a double recursion is the standard recursive definition of the sequence of Fibonacci numbers

$$0, 1, 1, 2, 3, 5, 8, 13, 21, \ldots$$

Each is the sum of the previous two numbers in the sequence. The recursive definition is

$$F(n) = \begin{array}{ll} 0 & \text{if } n = 0 \\ 1 & \text{if } n = 1 \\ F(n{-}2) + F(n{-}1) & \text{if } n > 1 \end{array}$$

Here is the pattern of recursive calls made for the F(5) tree. (A tree is a mathematical structure composed of vertices and edges. Each call is a vertex in the tree. Edges represent a method invocation. The root of the tree is at the top of the diagram and it grows down. The height of the tree is the length of the longest path from the root. Trees will be discussed in greater depth later when a corresponding data structure is created.)

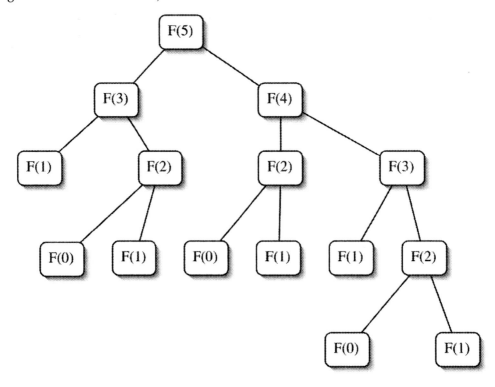

The problem with this is that the number of recursive calls made can grow exponentially as the tree of problems gets taller. Though it takes a bit of analysis to show, the number of invocations is exponential in n for this recursive definition of Fibonacci numbers.

One way of dealing with the exponential growth is to guarantee that the height of the tree grows slowly as the problem size increases. Accomplishing this requires that the size of the problem reduce quickly as you go down a branch in the tree. The merge sort algorithm, which will be presented later, guarantees this by solving two subproblems each of which is half the size of the original. Halving the size of the problems limits the height of the tree to $\log_2 n$.

The other way of dealing with the problem is to look for many instances of the same smaller problem. In those cases we can try two approaches. Memoization stores the results to problems when they are encountered for the first time. The next time a problem is seen, the result is just retrieved. The pattern for a memoized Fibonacci is shown next. An asterisk indicates the first evaluation. An underline indicates second evaluations. Base cases are just evaluated normally.

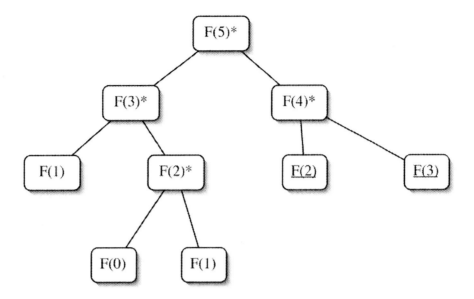

The other technique for dealing with this problem is to iteratively evaluate from small problems to larger problems. Note that for the Fibonacci sequence each number only depends on the previous two values, so you do not need to keep all the values. This results in the standard iterative algorithm for computing Fibonacci numbers.

Timing Programs

The different algorithms for computing Fibonacci numbers will be timed in this lab. This introduces a number of complications. To find the time, the following chunk of code will be used.

```
Calendar start = Calendar.getInstance();

// The Code being timed goes here

Calendar end   = Calendar.getInstance();
long diff      = end.getTime().getTime() -
          start.getTime().getTime();

System.out.println("Time to compute ... was "
          + diff + " milliseconds.");
```

Each time the getInstance() method is invoked, the current system time will be retrieved. That time is the number of milliseconds from some fixed date. One consequence of this is that the difference may be wrong by as much as a millisecond. Any time of that order is not to be trusted. With the speed of today's computers, some algorithms may complete well within that time frame. To address this issue, the code that is being timed may have a for loop that will execute the code multiple times. The reported time will be divided by the number of times the loop executes. This, of course, will introduce an extra time for the loop overhead, but it is assumed that this time will be small and can therefore be ignored.

Our timing difficulties are further complicated by the fact that the code being timed may not have been running the whole time. The Java Runtime Environment (JRE) is not the only program being executed. As the load on the computer changes, the amount of time the program gets will change as well. Running the same timing code with the same parameters will not give you the same result. You hope that the results are within 10%, but there is no guarantee. Another complicating factor is that the JRE is threaded. (Multiple tasks can be running each in their own thread within the JRE.) Some development environments will have threads running that will compete with your program's thread for time.

Another issue is that as computers get faster, the time required for the algorithms will decrease. This presents some problems in the instructions for the labs. An appropriate number of times to execute a loop today may be insufficient tomorrow. Two strategies have been used to ameliorate these problems.

The first strategy guarantees that enough iteration is done to get a reasonable execution time (usually on the order of a minute or so). The code is timed once for a fixed number of iterations. That time is then used to determine the number of iterations for the subsequent tests.

The second strategy addresses how to plot the times in a graph. Instead of plotting the actual time, a ratio is plotted instead. The ratio will be the actual time divided by a baseline time (usually the time for the smallest input). While the times themselves will vary from computer to computer, the ratios should be fairly stable.

Pre-Lab Visualization

Count

To start, consider a very simple recursion that does not do anything but count by ones. Each call of the recursion will be for a different value of count and has the responsibility of printing that value. The original call will be for the largest value to be printed.

First consider the problem of counting up. The smallest value that should be printed is 1. When doing the recursive design, think about whether the display should be done on the way down the recursion or on the way back up.

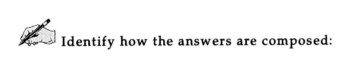 Identify the problem:

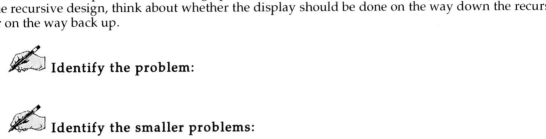 Identify the smaller problems:

Identify how the answers are composed:

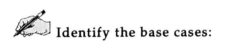 Identify the base cases:

Compose the recursive definition:

Show the operation of your definition on the number 4 in the following diagram. Inside the boxes, show the values of the arguments passed into the method. On the left-hand side, show the operations done before the recursive call by the method. On the right-hand side, show operations done after the recursive call.

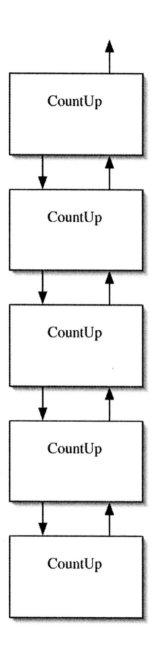

Now consider the problem of counting down. This should be very similar to the design of counting up.

✎ Identify the problem:

✎ Identify the smaller problems:

✎ Identify how the answers are composed:

✎ Identify the base cases:

✎ Compose the recursive definition:

Show the operation of your definition on the number 4 in the following diagram. Inside the boxes, show the values of the arguments passed into the method. On the left-hand side, show the operations done before the recursive call by the method. On the right-hand side, show operations done after the recursive call.

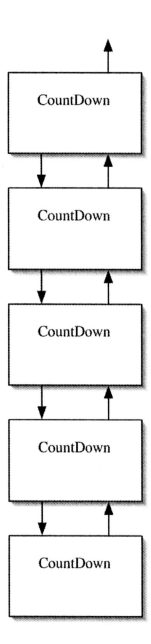

String Replace

Consider the problem of taking a String object and replacing every 'a' in the string with a 'b'. In general, the actual characters will be parameters of the replace method. The first problem you runs into is that a String is immutable. (Once a String object has been created, it cannot be changed.). So unlike an array, where the replace operation can be done in place, an approach more akin to the recursive reverse on a list is needed.

Examine the methods of the String class and show how you would implement them.

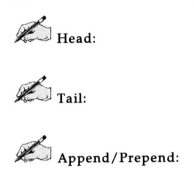 Head:

Tail:

Append/Prepend:

Using those methods and using reverse as a model complete the recursive design for the replace on a string.

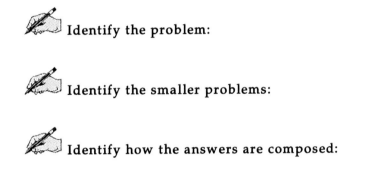 Identify the problem:

Identify the smaller problems:

Identify how the answers are composed:

Identify the base cases:

Compose the recursive definition:

Show the operation of your definition on the string "abcb" with 'b' replaced by 'e' in the following diagram. Inside the boxes, show the values of the arguments passed into the method. On the left-hand side, show the operations done before the recursive call by the method. On the right-hand side, show operations done after the recursive call and indicate what value is returned.

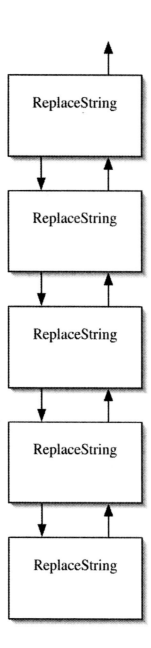

Tail Recursive Factorial

As is common with tail recursive designs, an extra variable for the partial solution needs to be added. Factorial will call a helper method that will do the actual recursion. Think about what factorial is computing in conjunction with the value of n that is available as one goes down the recursion.

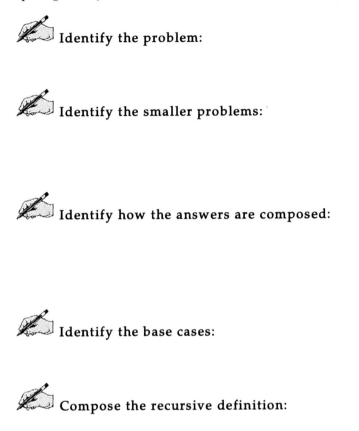 Identify the problem:

Identify the smaller problems:

Identify how the answers are composed:

Identify the base cases:

Compose the recursive definition:

Show the operation of your definition on the number 4 in the following diagram. In the boxes, show the values of the arguments passed into the method. On the left-hand side, show the operations done before the recursive call by the method. On the right-hand side, show operations done after the recursive call and indicate what value is returned.

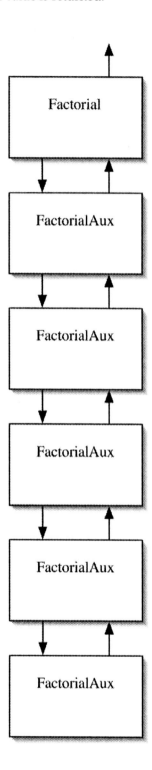

Improving Fibonacci

As was mentioned in the Introduction, one way of controlling a double recursion is to limit the height of the recursion tree. The standard recursive definition for Fibonacci numbers only reduces the problem size by one and two. This results in a tree that has height n. To control the height, you must define the recursion in terms of much smaller problem sizes.

Consider the values of F(n) in the following table.

n	F(n)
0	0
1	1
2	1
3	2
4	3
5	5
6	8
7	13
8	21
9	34
10	55
11	89
12	144
13	233
14	377

If the value of F(2n) can be related to the value of F(n), the problem size will be reduced in half and the growth of the tree will be tamed. In the following table, write down the numerical relation between F(n) and F(2n).

n	F(n)	F(2n)	Relation between F(n) and F(2n)
1	1	1	
2	1	3	
3	2	8	
4	3	21	
5	5	55	
6	8	144	
7	13	377	

Perhaps there is a pattern here. Clearly, though F(2n) does not depend on just F(n). Since Fibonacci is double recursion, perhaps the values depend on values that neighbor F(n). In the following table, write down the numerical relation.

n	F(n–1)	F(n)	F(n+1)	F(2n)	Relation between F(n–1), F(n), F(n+1) and F(2n)
1	0	1	1	1	
2	1	1	2	3	
3	1	2	3	8	
4	2	3	5	21	
5	3	5	8	55	
6	5	8	13	144	
7	8	13	21	377	

What simple formula does this relation follow?

While the values in the tables are a good sign of a relationship, by itself it is not concrete evidence. It is possible that the relation fails for larger values of n. A proof by mathematical induction of the discovered formula is required and can be done.

The F(n+1) term in the formula can be eliminated to produce:

$$F(2n) = F^2(n) + 2F(n)F(n{-}1)$$

While this definition works for even values, what about odd values? Starting with the formula:

$$F(2n{+}2) = F(2n{+}1) + F(2n)$$

one can derive
$$F(2n{+}1) = 2F^2(n) + 2F(n)F(n{-}1) + F^2(n{-}1)$$

This results in the recursive definition:

$$F(n)= \begin{cases} 0 & n=0 \\ 1 & n=1 \\ F^2(n/2) + 2F(n/2)F(n/2{-}1) & n \text{ is even and } > 1 \\ 2F^2(n/2) + 2F(n/2)F(n/2{-}1) + F^2(n/2{-}1) & n \text{ is odd and } > 1 \end{cases}$$

Show the pattern of calls for F(17) and record the values produced by each call.

What is the height of the tree for F(n)?

How many recursive calls are made? Express your answer in big-O notation.

Tail Recursive Fibonacci

Note that the previous recursive formulation has repeated subproblems. Therefore, memoization or an iterative formulation can improve the performance even more. Notice, however, that not all possible subproblems need to be computed. To compute from the bottom, the needed subproblems have to be identified.

Consider the following two partial trees.

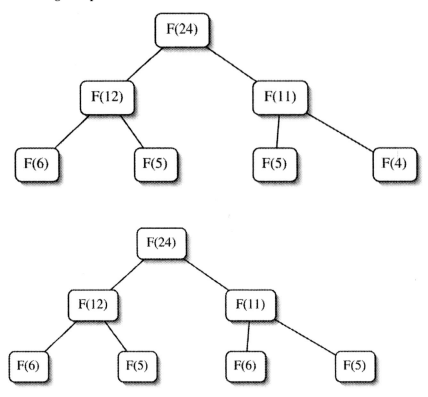

Looking at the third line, the first tree depends on three different problems, while the second only depends on two problems. The second tree is more desirable in that it has fewer problems it repeats. The first tree needs to be fixed so that only two values are needed at each level of the tree.

The problem arises when the larger of the two values needed is even. What is desired is a definition of F(2n–1) in terms of F(n) and F(n–1). Looking at the definitions for F(2n) and F(2n+1) and recalling that any Fibonacci number is the sum of the previous two, it is easy to derive a definition.

$$F(2n-1) = F^2(n) + F^2(n-1)$$
$$F(2n) = F^2(n) + 2F(n)F(n-1)$$
$$F(2n+1) = 2F^2(n) + 2F(n)F(n-1) + F^2(n-1)$$

Using the relation for F(2n–1) for F(11) in the first tree gives:

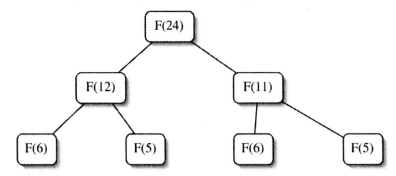

Now each level in the tree will only have two values. The two values needed on the next level are determined by larger n value on the level above. If it is even, use the formulas:

$$F(2n) = F^2(n) + 2F(n)F(n-1)$$
$$F(2n-1) = F^2(n) + F^2(n-1)$$

If it is odd, use the formulas

$$F(2n+1) = 2F^2(n) + 2F(n)F(n-1) + F^2(n-1)$$
$$F(2n) = F^2(n) + 2F(n)F(n-1)$$

The only remaining problem is to determine which pairs of Fibonacci numbers will be computed for a given n.

Write down the pairs needed for n=50.

Suppose n is 163. Each of the pairs is recorded in the following table. The values will depend on the bits in 163. To the right is the bit pattern for 163. Circle the bit that is associated with each pair. Indicate which pair of formulas was used to get that row from the row below.

F(81)	F(80)	1 0 1 0 0 0 1 1	
F(40)	F(39)	1 0 1 0 0 0 1 1	
F(20)	F(19)	1 0 1 0 0 0 1 1	
F(10)	F(9)	1 0 1 0 0 0 1 1	
F(5)	F(4)	1 0 1 0 0 0 1 1	
F(2)	F(1)	1 0 1 0 0 0 1 1	
F(1)	F(0)	1 0 1 0 0 0 1 1	

What pair is always at the bottom?

Which bit determines the row for F(2) and F(1)?

If the determining bit is even, which pair of formulas is used?

It is now time to design the tail recursive method for Fibonacci numbers. Again, a tail recursive helper method will be used. This time, however, two partial solutions are required (one for each of the pair of values). The bits in n will determine the pattern of values. Two extra methods will be needed. The first will get the second most significant bit (the bit to the right of the most significant bit) of a number n. The second will remove the second most significant bit from a number n.

Consider the number 5. It has the bit pattern 101_2. The second bit from the left is 0. Removing the 0 gives 11_2, which is 3.

What are the bit patterns for 96, 95, 16, 15, and 9?

Give an algorithm to find the second most significant bit in a number n.

Verify that it works on the bit patterns for 96, 95, 16, 15, and 9.

Give an algorithm to return the value found by removing the second most significant bit in a number n.

Verify that it works on the previous bit patterns.

Using the methods secondMSB() and reduceBySecondMSB(), design a tail recursive algorithm for Fibonacci numbers.

 Identify the problem:

 Identify the smaller problems:

 Identify how the answers are composed:

 Identify the base cases:

 Compose the recursive definition:

Does your definition work for n=0?

Does your definition work for n=1?

Show the operation of your definition on the number 14 in the following diagram. Inside the boxes, show the values of the arguments passed into the method. On the left-hand side, show the operations done before the recursive call by the method. On the right-hand side, show operations done after the recursive call and indicate what value is returned.

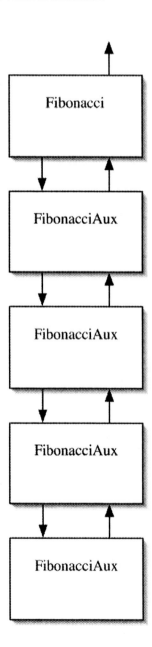

Directed Lab Work

Count

The first goal of this lab is to implement a couple of simple recursive methods that do not compute or return anything. Their sole purpose is to print integer values.

Step 1. Look at the skeleton in *Count.java*. Compile and run the `main` method in `Count`.

Checkpoint: The program will ask you for an integer value. Enter any value. A couple messages will be displayed, but no counting will happen.

Step 2. Refer to the count up recursive design from the Pre-Lab Exercises. Complete the recursive method `countUp()`.

Checkpoint: Run Count. For the integer value enter 5. You should see 1 2 3 4 5.

Step 3. Refer to the count down recursive design from the Pre-Lab Exercises. Complete the recursive method `countDown()`.

Final checkpoint: Run Count. For the integer value enter 5. You should see 5 4 3 2 1.

String Replace

The next goal is to complete a recursive method that will replace all occurrences of a given character with another character.

Step 1. Compile and run the `main` method in `TestReplace`.

Checkpoint: The program will run and get a null pointer exception.

Step 2. Refer to the string replace recursive design from the Pre-Lab Exercises and complete the method `replace()` in *RecursiveStringReplace.java..*

Final Checkpoint: Compile and run TestReplace. All tests should pass.

Tail Recursive Factorial

The next goal is to complete a tail recursive helper method that will compute the factorial function.

Step 1. Compile and run the `main` method in `TestFactorial`.

Checkpoint: The program will run and fail most tests.

Step 2. Refer to the recursive design from the Pre-Lab Exercises and complete the methods `tailRecursive()` and `helper()` in *RecursiveFactorial.java*.

Final Checkpoint: Compile and run TestFactorial. All tests should pass.

Timing Basic Fibonacci

The next goal is to see how long it takes to compute Fibonacci numbers using the basic recursive formulation.

Step 1. Compile `TimeFibonacci`.

Step 2. Run the code for even values of n and record the first value of n for which the time is greater than 100 milliseconds. (24 is a good place to start your search. Avoid large values.)

FIRST EVEN VALUE OF N FOR WHICH THE TIME OF BASIC FIBONACCI IS GREATER THAN 100 MILLISECONDS	X =

Step 3. Fill in the values for *n* in the following table. Run the program and fill in the times. Stop timing when the time is longer than 100,000 milliseconds (about 2 minutes).

N	TIME IN MILLISECONDS TO COMPUTE F(N) USING THE BASIC FIBONACCI RECURSION
X =	
X+ 2 =	
X+ 4 =	
X+ 6 =	
X+ 8 =	
X+ 10 =	
X+ 12 =	
X+ 14 =	
X+ 16 =	
X+ 18 =	
X+ 20 =	
X+ 22 =	
X+ 24 =	
X+ 26 =	
X+ 28 =	
X+ 30 =	

Step 4. Plot points from the preceding table on the following graph. Don't worry about plotting the points that are off the graph.

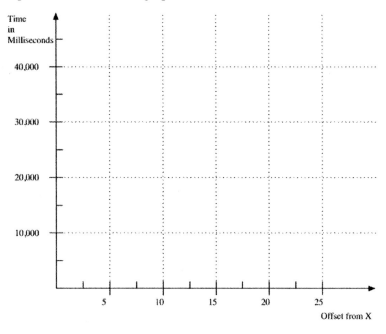

Step 5. Draw a smooth curve that approximates the points.

A Better Version of Fibonacci

The next goal is to implement the better versions of factorial that were discovered in the Pre-Lab Exercises. They will be timed.

Step 6.   Refer to the Pre-Lab Exercise and complete the implementation of the method `better()` in `RecursiveFibonacci`.

Step 7.   Compile `TestFibonacci`.

Checkpoint: Run `TestFibonacci`. All tests for the better Fibonacci formulation should pass.

A Tail Recursive Version of Fibonacci

Step 8.   Refer to the recursive formulation from Improving Fibonacci in the Pre-Lab and complete the implementation of the method `secondMSB()` in `RecursiveFibonacci`. Don't forget to change the return statement.

Step 9.   Refer to the recursive formulation from Improving Fibonacci in the Pre-Lab Exercises and complete the implementation of the method `reduceBy2ndMSB()` in `RecursiveFibonacci`.

Step 10.   Test the two methods you just created.

Step 11.   Refer to the recursive formulation from Improving Fibonacci in the Pre-Lab Exercises and create a tail recursive helper method in `RecursiveFibonacci` that uses `secondMSB()` and `reduceBy2ndMSB()`.

Step 12.   Complete the method `tailRecursive()` in `RecursiveFibonacci` that calls the tail recursive helper method you created.

Step 13.   Compile `TestFibonacci`.

Checkpoint: Run `TestFibonacci`. All tests for the both Fibonacci formulations should pass.

More Timing of Fibonacci

Step 14.   Comment out the call to `timeBasic()` in `TimeFibonacci`.

Step 15.   Uncomment the code to time the better and tail recursive versions of Fibonacci in `TimeFibonacci`.

Step 16.   Run `TimeFibonacci`. Enter 100 for n and 10000 for the number of trials. Fill in the value in the table.

TIME IN MILLISECONDS TO COMPUTE F(100) USING THE BETTER RECURSIVE FORMULA	T =

Step 17.   Complete the following computation.

TRIALS = 10000 / T =

Step 18. Fill in the following table. Use TRIALS for the number of trials.

	TIME IN MILLISECONDS FOR BETTER FIBONACCI	TIME IN MILLISECONDS FOR TAIL RECURSIVE FIBONACCI
n=10		
n=20		
n=30		
n=40		
n=50		
n=60		
n=70		
n=80		
n=90		
n=100		

Step 19. Plot points (in different colors) for the times for two different versions of Fibonacci in the table. Put appropriate value labels on the *y*-axis of the graph.

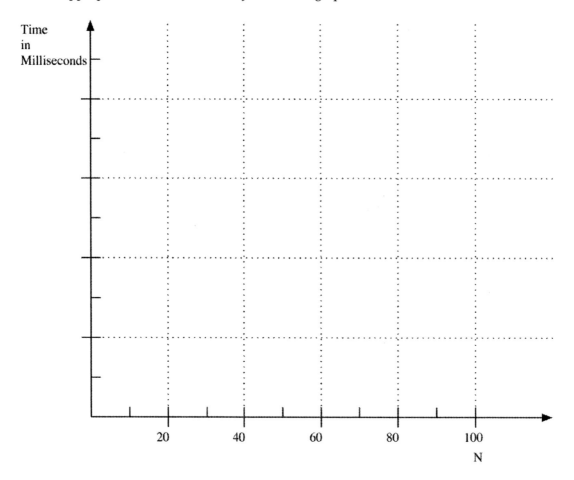

Note that even though the better formulation allows computations for larger values of N in terms of time, the size of the values is still problematic. The methods all use the long data type and will quickly overflow.

Post-Lab Follow-Ups

1. Develop a recursive algorithm for computing the product of a sequence of odd values. Use that method to develop a recursive algorithm for factorial that splits the problem into a product of even values and a product of odd values.

2. Develop a recursive algorithm that given a and n, computes the sum:

   $$S = 1 + a + a^2 + ... + a^n$$

3. Develop a recursive algorithm similar to string replace which works in place on an array of characters.

4. Develop a recursive algorithm for computing the second most significant bit of a number n.

5. Develop a recursive algorithm for computing the result of removing the second most significant bit from a number n.

6. Look at the ratio of the times for computing Fibonacci numbers F(n) and F(n+2) using the basic recursive formula. Given that you know how long it would take to compute F(X), predict the amount of time it would take to compute F(X+50). Predict the amount of time it would take to compute F(X+100).

7. Write a loop to compute successive values of F(n) using the tail recursive version. For what value of n does the computation overflow?

Lab 7   Recursion—Part II

Goal

The exploration of recursion is continued in this lab with a focus on double recursion. Two applications will be developed. The first is the Reve's problem, which is similar to the towers of Hanoi puzzle, and the second computes the maximum of an array.

Resources

- Chapter 10: Recursion
- *Hanoi.jar*—Sample application: Towers of Hanoi on four poles
- *Reves.jar*—Sample application: The Reve's puzzle
- *Disk.html*— Interface documentation for *Disk.java*
- *Pole.html*—Interface documentation for *Pole.java*
- Appendix A—The Animated Application Framework

Java Files

- *BadArgumentsForMaxException.java*
- *RecursiveMaxOfArray.java*
- *TestMax.java*

Files in Directory *RevesApplication*:
- *Disk.java*
- *Pole.java*
- *RevesActionThread.java*
- *RevesApplication.java*
- Other framework classes discussed in Appendix A

Introduction

One of the classic examples of a doubly recursive algorithm is the solution to the towers of Hanoi. There are three poles and n disks of different sizes. The disks are stacked on one of the poles and are to be moved another pole. There are two basic rules. First, only one disk can be moved at a time. Second, no disk can be moved on top of a smaller disk.

Identify the problem:
Hanoi(n, from, to, extra)

Identify the smaller problems:
With four disks to be moved from pole A to pole C, the puzzle starts with the following picture.

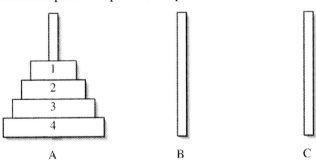

If the disks from 1 through 3 could be moved off of pole A, the largest disk would be free to move. The stack of three disks must all be moved onto pole B, or C will not be available for disk 4. Once this has been done, disks 1 through 3 must then be moved onto pole C.

There are two smaller problems to be solved.

        Hanoi(n–1, from, extra, to)
and
        Hanoi(n–1, extra, to, from)

Identify how the answers are composed:

    Hanoi(n, from, to, extra) is
            1.   Hanoi(n–1, from, extra, to)
            2.   Move disk n off pole *from* onto pole *to*.
            3.   Hanoi(n–1, extra, to, from)

Identify the base cases:

There are two possibilities for the base case. Either n is 0 or n is 1. Certainly, if *n* is zero, nothing needs to be done. If *n* is 1, one disk needs to be moved. Either one will give a satisfactory base case.

        Hanoi(0, from, to, extra) is
            1. Do nothing.

Compose the recursive definition:

Hanoi(n, from, to, extra) is
        If n =0
                1. Do nothing.
        If n > 0
            1.   Hanoi(n–1, from, extra, to)
            2.   Move disk n off pole *from* onto pole *to*
            3.   Hanoi(n–1, extra, to, from)

The tree for three disks is shown here.

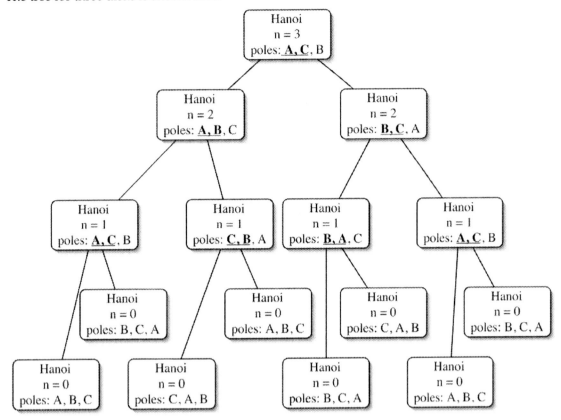

The move made by each recursive call is indicated by underlining the poles involved in the move.

The second application is known as the Reve's puzzle. It is a game that is similar to the towers of Hanoi puzzle. The only difference is that there are four poles instead of three. For the towers of Hanoi, it is known that the recursive algorithm will move the disks optimally (in the least number of moves). Of the algorithms that solve the Reve's puzzle, it is not known which, if any, is optimal. There is a conjecture that the Frame-Stewart algorithm, which will be used in the lab, gives the optimum.

Pre-Lab Visualization

The Reve's Puzzle

The Frame-Stewart algorithm for the Reve's puzzle will use the solution to the towers of Hanoi.

Suppose you need to move n disks from pole 1 to pole 4, with poles 2 and 3 as extras. If there is a single disk, Frame-Stewart will just move the disk, from pole 1 to pole 4. If there is more than one disk the algorithm has 3 steps. First, recursively move the top n–k disks from pole 1 to pole 2. Second, move the remaining k disks from pole 1 to 4, using the towers of Hanoi algorithm on just poles 1, 3, and 4. Last, recursively move the n–k disks from pole 2 to 4.

This is similar in structure to the towers of Hanoi, except that in the middle step more than one disk is moved.

The value of k is chosen to be the smallest integer value where n does not exceed k(k+1)/2 (the kth triangular number).

Fill in the following table with the values of the triangular numbers.

K	K(K+1)/2
1	
2	
3	
4	
5	
6	
7	

For each n, find the k value such that n does not exceed the kth triangular number from the preceding table.

N	SMALLEST K WHERE N IS NOT GREATER THAN K(K+1)/2
1	
2	
3	
4	
5	
6	
7	
8	
9	
10	
11	

Give an algorithm to compute k given n.

Using the operation to compute k, complete the recursive design for the Reve's puzzle.

Identify the problem:

Identify the smaller problems:

Identify how the answers are composed:

Identify the base cases:

Compose the recursive definition:

Trace the operation of your algorithm for n=4. The solution should have nine moves.

Maximum

This application will compute the maximum value in an array. It will split the array into halves and thus avoid an exponential performance cost. The pattern of this recursion is similar to what will be seen later for the advanced sorting algorithms.

As with the other recursive algorithms that work on an array, a range of values in the array will be examined. This range will be split in half.

To start consider how the split will be made. Suppose the recursive algorithm is asked to look at the portion of an array that ranges from 3 to 9.

INDEX	...	3	4	5	6	7	8	9	...
VALUE		20	40	10	90	50	70	80	

How many values are there in the range?

What is the index of the middle value in the range?

If the limits of the range are *first* and *last,* give a formula to compute the index of the middle value.

The task now is to split up the array, but where should the middle value go? It can either go in the first half, the second half, or neither half. To answer this question, consider a portion of the array with just two elements. This is the smallest range that can be split up and is a useful test case. If this case does not work, the recursive algorithm is doomed to failure.

Using the preceding formula, what will be the index of the middle value?

In the following arrays, box the left and right halves for the given condition.

 Middle in first half:

INDEX	...	3	4	...
VALUE		20	40	

 Middle in second half:

INDEX	...	3	4	...
VALUE		20	40	

 Middle in neither half:

INDEX	...	3	4	...
VALUE		20	40	

What is the maximum of an empty range? This is problematic. The maximum is not defined in that situation. Only one of the three cases will have a nonempty for both of the halves.

If the limits of the range are *first* and *last* and middle is the middle index, what are the ranges for the first and second halves?

 First half range:

 Second half range:

Having thought about how to split the range in half, continue on with the recursive design.

 Identify the problem:

Identify the smaller problems:

 Identify how the answers are composed:

 Identify the base cases:

 Compose the recursive definition:

Show the operation of your definition on the array [9 3 4 5 7] with the range of 0 to 4 on the following diagram. Inside the boxes, show the values of the arguments passed into the method. On the left-hand side, show the operations done before the recursive call by the method. On the right-hand side, show operations done after the recursive call. There are two more recursive calls that will be made but are not shown in the picture. Their location will depend on how the split was formulated. Add them in.

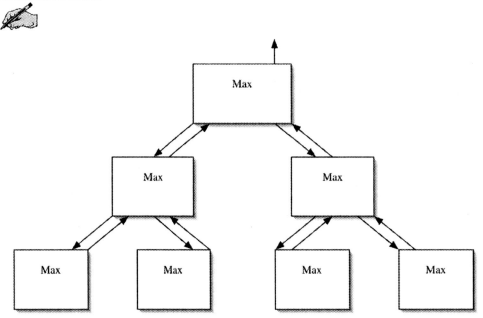

Directed Lab Work

Reve's Puzzle

The first part of the lab is to complete an animated application that solves the Reve's puzzle. Approximately half of the classes in the application implement the framework that animates the application. A description of the classes in the framework is given in Appendix A. For the most part, these classes can be ignored as the animated application is developed as long as appropriate care is taken. The appendix also gives instructions for using the framework to create new animated applications.

Step 1. Compile all the classes in the folder `RevesApplication`. Run the `main` method in `AnimatedReves`.

Checkpoint: The program will run and a graphical user interface will appear. Across the top will be controls for stepping the application. At this point there are only two steps that can be done. Step from the setup phase to the initial state. Then step to the final state. At this point reset must be pressed. Do so. Pressing the go button will automatically step the application to the final state. The speed of the steps is controlled by the speed text field and can be changed at any time. The smaller the number is the quicker the steps will be. The default speed of 100 corresponds to 1 second. Pause can be pressed at any time and the application can be single stepped again.

In the setup phase, the number of disks can be changed. Enter a value into the text field and press enter. Once step is pressed and the application is in the initial state, the number of disks cannot be changed during the current execution of the application. (You can always press reset to abort the current execution and go back to the setup phase.)

The first goal is to create the disks and poles that the application will use.

Step 2. If you have not already, look at the interface documentation in *Pole.html* and *Disk.html*.

Step 3. In the `init()` method of `RevesActionThread`, add code to create four poles and assign them to the variables a, b, c, and d.

Step 4. Add code that creates the disks and puts them on pole a.

Checkpoint: Compile the classes and run AnimatedReves. There should be four poles and 10 disks on the first pole. Type 4 in the text field for the number of disks and press enter. The number of disks displayed should change.

The next goal is to complete the code that will move a disk from one pole to another.

Step 5. Examine the method `moveDisk()` in `RevesActionThread`. It already has code that displays the move in the window and waits for a step. Don't change this code.

Step 6. Add code that will remove the top disk from one pole and then add it to the other pole.

Step 7. In the `executeApplication()` method of `RevesActionThread`, add the line of code

```
moveDisk(a,b);
```

Checkpoint: Compile the classes and run AnimatedReves. Step three times. The top disk on pole a should move to pole b.

The next goal is to create the code that will solve the towers of Hanoi.

Step 8. Refer to the recursive design from the Pre-Lab Exercises and create the method `towersOfHanoi()` in `RevesActionThread`. Make sure you call the `moveDisk()` method that was just completed.

Step 9. Change the single line of code in the `executeApplication()` method of `RevesActionThread` to call `towersOfHanoi()`. The source pole will be a, the destination will be d, and the extra will be b. Use the variable `disks` for the number of disks to move.

Checkpoint: Compile the classes and run AnimatedReves. The application should move the disks as expected. You may run Hanoi.jar to see what it should look like.

The final goal is to complete the Frame-Stewart algorithm.

Step 10. Refer to the algorithm for finding the value of k and create a method to compute it in RevesActionThread.

Step 11. Refer to the recursive design from the Pre-Lab Exercises and create the method reves() in RevesActionThread. Make sure to call the method that was just completed in the previous step.

Step 12. Change the single line of code in the executeApplication() method of RevesActionThread to call reves(). The source pole will be a, the destination will be d, and the extras will be b and c. Use the variable disks for the number of disks to move.

Final checkpoint: Compile the classes and run AnimatedReves.

Try the application with three disks. It should use five moves.

Try the application with four disks. It should use nine moves.

The application should move the disks as expected. You may run to Reves.jar to see what it should look like.

Maximum

The second part of the lab is to complete the maximum application.

Step 1. Look at the skeleton in *RecursiveMaxOfArray.java*. Compile and run the main method in TestMax.

Checkpoint: The program should run and fail all tests.

Step 2. Refer to the recursive design from the Pre-Lab Exercises. Complete the recursive method max(). Don't forget to throw an exception if there is not at least one value in the range.

Final checkpoint: Run TestMax. All tests should pass.

Post-Lab Follow-Ups

1. Determine the number of moves that the towers of Hanoi and the Reve's puzzles take for 1 to 15 disks. Plot the number of moves versus the number of disks.

2. Develop and implement a recursive algorithm to solve the Reve's puzzle that recursively moves half the disks to one of the extra posts, then moves all but the bottom disk to the other extra post (using only three posts). Move the bottom disk to the destination. Move the other two stacks of disks appropriately. Compare the number of moves needed compared to the Frame-Stewart algorithm.

3. Develop a recursive algorithm to move n disks from a source pole to a destination pole using three extra poles (five poles total).

4. *For those who are familiar with drawing in Java.* Make a copy of your solution to the Reve's puzzle and modify it to use five poles. Implement your algorithm from the previous question.

5. Develop code to time the performance of the recursive maximum. Plot the performance and identify the time complexity of the solution.

6. Develop and implement a doubly recursive algorithm for computing the product of all the values in an array.

7. Develop and implement a doubly recursive algorithm that moves the minimum value to the beginning of an array.

Lab 8   Basic Sorts

Goal

In this lab the performance of basic sorting algorithms will be explored.

Resources

- Chapter 11: An Introduction to Sorting

Java Files

- *SortArray.java*
- *SortDriver.java*

Introduction

Sorting is an important basic operation used by many applications. A lot of effort has been spent creating fast sorting algorithms. In this lab, the performance of three basic sorting algorithms will be measured. Since better algorithms are known, these algorithms are of limited use. (The performance of two faster algorithms, merge sort and quick sort, will be examined in the next lab.)

One of the difficulties in measuring the performance of the Fibonacci computation was that different computers execute at different speeds. One method for dealing with this problem is to find a core operation that the algorithm performs. The performance of the algorithm will be determined in terms of the number of times that operation is performed. This will give a way of comparing two algorithms that is independent of the computer the algorithm runs on.

For general purpose sorting algorithms, the standard measure is the number of comparisons that are made.

The Statistics

To get a fair view of the performance of a sort, it is not enough to just try it on one array. Instead, it should be tested on a number of randomly generated arrays $A_1, A_2, A_3, \dots A_k$. For each array, the number of comparisons made will be counted giving $C_1, C_2, C_3, \dots C_k$. From these data values, the average, minimum, and maximum number of comparisons will be computed.

The computed average number of comparisons will give an approximation to the true average number of comparisons used by the algorithm. Assuming that the generation of the arrays is truly random, larger values for k will lead to a closer approximation to the true average.

The minimum and maximum give an indication of how consistent the performance is. They also give a rough indication of what the best and worst cases, respectively, are. Be aware, though, that the number of possible orderings of an array is n factorial. If relatively few of the cases lead to best- or worst-case behavior, they are unlikely to show up in the randomly chosen test cases.

In practice, the worst and average cases are of interest. The worst case allows you to guarantee the performance of an algorithm. On the other hand, if the algorithm is going to be used many times, the possibility of the worst case may be tolerated to achieve better overall performance.

Pre-Lab Visualization

Computing Statistics

Consider an object, which is given the values $C_1, C_2, C_3, \ldots C_k$ one at a time. In other words, it has a method giveValue(c). It is not allowed to keep the values in an array, but it can have a limited number of private variables. After each call to the method giveValue(), the object is required to know the current minimum, maximum, and average.

What private variables should it use?

Create an algorithm for giveValue(c).

Test it on the sequence:

giveValue(-10)

Test it on the sequence:

giveValue(7)

Test it on the sequence:

giveValue(3)
giveValue(2)
giveValue(-5)
giveValue(10)
giveValue(33)
giveValue(1)

Predicting the Average Performance of Selection Sort

In selection sort, the array is divided in two parts. The first part has sorted values. The second part has values that are in arbitrary order. All the values in the first part are less than the values in the second part. At each phase of the algorithm, the smallest value in the second part is found (selected) and swapped to the end of the first part.

The following picture shows the state of selection sort at an intermediate step.

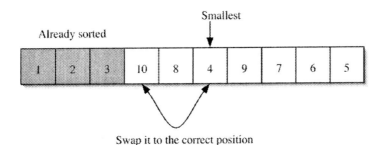

Suppose someone told you the position of the smallest value in the second portion of the array. How many values must be checked to verify that 4 is the smallest value? (Does 4 need to be checked against itself?)

While this is not the way selection sort finds the 4, it does give a minimum for the number of comparisons required. In fact, selection sort will use that number of comparisons.

The general case of n values:
How many comparisons are needed in the first pass if there are n values?

How many comparisons are needed in the second pass if there are n values?

How many comparisons are needed in the third pass if there are n values?

What is the sequence of comparisons needed?

What is the sum of the sequence?

For n=20, how many comparisons are required?

Remember this value for the lab.

Predicting the Average Performance of Insertion Sort

In insertion sort, the array is again divided into two parts. The first part has sorted values. The second part has values that are in arbitrary order. Unlike selection sort, the values in the first part may be larger than values in the second part. At each phase of the algorithm, the next value in the unsorted part is inserted into the correct place in the sorted part.

The following picture shows the state of insertion sort at an intermediate step.

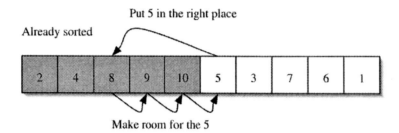

What is the largest number of values that the 5 must be checked against?

What is the smallest number of values that the 5 must be checked against?

If all values from the largest to smallest are equally possible, what is the average number of comparisons?

The general case of n values:
It is easier to think about the phases of insertion sort in reverse order.

What is the average number of comparisons needed in the last pass if there are n values?

What is the average number of comparisons needed in the second to last pass if there are n values?

What is the average number of comparisons needed in the third to last pass if there are n values?

What is the average number of comparisons needed in the third pass if there are n values? (3 items already in the sorted part.)

What is the average number of comparisons needed in the second pass if there are n values? (2 items already in the sorted part.)

What is the average number of comparisons needed in the first pass if there are n values? (1 item already in the sorted part.)

What is the sequence of comparisons needed?

What is the sum of the sequence?

For n=20, how many comparisons are required on average?

Remember this value for the lab.

Directed Lab Work

The basic sorts have been implemented in the SortArray class. You will make a new class SortArrayInstrumented that will be based on that class. It will allow you to gather statistics about the sorts. The SortDriver class will generate the arrays, call the sorts, and then display the statistical results.

Adding Statistics to Selection Sort

Step 1. If you have not done so, look at the implementation of the sorts in *SortArray.java*. Look at the skeleton in *SortDriver.java*. Compile the classes SortArray, and SortDriver. Run the main method in SortDriver.

Checkpoint: The program will ask you for an array size. Enter 20. An array of 20 random values between 0 and 20 should be generated and displayed. Selection sort will be applied to array and the sorted array will be displayed. Verify that this works correctly.

The first goal is to create a new class SortArrayInstrumented that will be used to collect statistics about the performance of the sorts. Private variables of the class will be used to record the number of comparisons made.

Step 2. Create a new class name SortArrayInstrumented.

Step 3. Copy the contents of SortArray into SortArrayInstrumented. Change the name in the class declaration from SortArray to SortArrayInstrumented.

Step 4. Create a default constructor that does nothing. (It will have work to do later.)

Step 5. Remove static from all the methods in the SortArrayInstrumented class.

Checkpoint: You should be able to compile SortArrayInstrumented without errors.

Since the sort methods are no longer static, SortDriver must be changed to create an instance of SortArrayInstrumented and then invoke the sort method using the instance.

Step 6. In main of sortDriver declare and create a new instance of SortArrayInstrumented named sai.

Step 7. Change SortArray.selectionSort(data, arraySize) to sai.selectionSort(data, arraySize).

Checkpoint: Compile and run the program. Enter 20 for the array size. Verify that this works correctly.

The next goal is to add code to the selection sort to count the number of times that a comparison of data values is made. Methods will be added to the SortArrayInstrumented class to allow the number of comparisons to be recovered.

Step 8. Add a private variable comparisons of type long to the SortArrayInstrumented class. Initialize it to zero in the constructor.

Step 9. Add a public accessor method getComparisons to the SortArrayInstrumented class.

Step 10. In order to count the number of times that compareTo() is called by selection sort, put the line

    comparisons++;

just before the if statement in indexOfSmallest(). If the code is inserted inside the then clause, only the comparisons that result in true will be counted.

Step 11. Add a public accessor method getComparisons to the SortArrayInstrumented class.

Step 12. In SortDriver, add the line

    System.out.println("   comparison made: "+sai.getComparisons());

after the call to selection sort.

Checkpoint: Compile and run the program. Enter 20 for the array size. Verify that the sort still works correctly. The number of comparisons should be 190.

The next goal is to compute the average number of comparisons made by the sort with many different lists (all of the same size). Only SortDriver will be changed.

Step 13. In SortDriver, use the method getInt() to set the variable trials.

Step 14. Starting with the call to generateRandomArray, wrap the remainder of the code in main in SortDriver with a for loop that runs the given number of trials.

Checkpoint: Compile and run the program. Enter 20 for the array size. Enter 3 for the number of trials. Verify that each of the three sorts works correctly and is for a different list of 20 values. The number of comparisons should be 190, 380, and 570.

Notice that the number of comparisons gives a running total for all calls. The next goal is to compute and report the minimum and maximum number of comparisons made over all the calls to the sort. To do this, the use of the comparisons variable will be changed slightly. It will only be the number of comparisons made by the last call to the sort. The total number of comparisons made by all calls will be held in a new variable. This aids in the computation of the maximum and minimum.

Step 15. Add a private variable totalComparisons of type long to the SortArrayInstrumented class. Initialize it to zero in the constructor.

Step 16. Add a private variable minComparisons of type long to the SortArrayInstrumented class. Initialize it to Long.MAX_VALUE in the constructor.

Step 17. Add a private variable maxComparisons of type long to the SortArrayInstrumented class. Initialize it to zero in the constructor.

Step 18. Add three public accessor methods (one for each of the new variables) to the SortArrayInstrumented class.

To compute the minimum and maximum number of comparisons, code needs to be added at the beginning and end of the sort. While the needed code could be added directly to the sorts, it is better to encapsulate it in a couple new methods.

Step 19. Add a private method startStatistics() to the SortArrayInstrumented class. It should initialize comparisons to zero.

Step 20. Add a private method endStatistics() to the SortArrayInstrumented class. It should add comparisons to totalComparisons. It should compare comparisons to minComparisons and set minComparisons to whichever is smaller. It should also set maxComparisons in an analogous fashion.

Step 21. Call startStatistics() at the beginning of the selectionSort method. Call endStatistics() at the end of the selectionSort method.

Step 22. After the `for` loop in `main` of `SortDriver`, add in three statements that print the total, minimum, and maximum number of comparisons.

Checkpoint: Compile and run the program. Enter 20 for the array size. Enter 3 for the number of trials. Verify that each of the three sorts works correctly and is for a different list of 20 values. The number of comparisons should be 190 for each of the three calls. The total should be 570 and the minimum and maximum should both be 190. Refer to the Pre-Lab Exercises and compare.

Enter 10 for the array size. Enter 3 for the number of trials. Verify that each of the three sorts works correctly and is for a different list of 10 values. The number of comparisons should be 45 for each of the three calls. The total should be 135 and the minimum and maximum should both be 45.

Step 23. Compute the average number of comparisons made over the trials and print it. (The average is the total number of comparisons divided by the number of trials.)

Step 24. In preparation for filling in the table, comment out the print statements inside the `for` loop in `main`.

Final checkpoint: Compile and run the program. Enter 20 for the array size. Enter 1000 for the number of trials. The total should be 19000 and the average, minimum, and maximum should all be 190.

Step 25. Fill in this table and the appropriate column in the table at the end of the directed lab. Use 100 trials.

Comparisons for Selection Sort

	MINIMUM COMPARISONS	AVERAGE COMPARISONS	MAXIMUM COMPARISONS
Size=10			
Size=50			
Size=100			
Size=200			
Size=300			
Size=400			
Size=500			
Size=750			
Size=1000			

Adding Statistics to Insertion Sort

Most of the work needed has been done before. It is now just a matter of adding the appropriate code to the insertion sort code.

Step 26. Add calls to `startStatistics()` and `endStatistics()` to the public, nonrecursive `insertionSort()` method.

Step 27. In the `insertionSort()` method place code to add one to comparisons when `compareTo()` is invoked.

Step 28. In `main` in `SortDriver`, change the call from `selectionSort` to `insertionSort`.

Step 29. Uncomment the print statements in the `for` loop in `main` in `SortDriver`.

Checkpoint: Compile and run the program. Enter 20 for the array size. Enter 3 for the number of trials. Verify that each of the three sorts works correctly and is for a different list of 20 values. The number of comparisons should be approximately 105 for each of the three calls. Verify that the total, minimum, and maximum are correct for the reported number of comparisons. Refer to the Pre-Lab Exercises and compare.

Enter 10 for the array size. Enter 3 for the number of trials. Verify that each of the three sorts works correctly and is for a different list of 10 values. The number of comparisons should be approximately 27 for each of the three calls. Verify that the total, minimum, and maximum are correct for the reported number of comparisons

Step 30. Recomment the `print` statements from the previous step.

Final checkpoint: Compile and run the program. Enter 20 for the array size. Enter 10000 for the number of trials. The average you get should be within the range of 101 to 108 approximately 99% of the time. If you get a value outside the range, retry the test a few times. If your result is consistently outside the range, check the code you added.

Step 31. Fill in this table and the appropriate column in the table at the end of the directed lab. Use 100 trials.

Comparisons for Insertion Sort

	MINIMUM COMPARISONS	AVERAGE COMPARISONS	MAXIMUM COMPARISONS
Size=10			
Size=50			
Size=100			
Size=200			
Size=300			
Size=400			
Size=500			
Size=750			
Size=1000			

Adding Statistics to Shell Sort

Step 1. Add calls to `startStatistics()` and `endStatistics()` to the public `shellSort()` method.

Step 2. In the `incrementalInsertionSort()` method place code to add one to comparisons when `compareTo()` is invoked. Since the comparison is in the end condition of a for loop, this is a bit trickier to account for than with the other two sorts. The `compareTo` method may have been called one more time than the number of times the body of the loop was executed.

Step 3. In `main` in `SortDriver`, change the call from `insertionSort` to `shellSort`.

Step 4. Uncomment the `print` statements in the `for` loop in `main` in `SortDriver`.

Checkpoint: Compile and run the program. Enter 20 for the array size. Enter 3 for the number of trials. Verify that each of the three sorts works correctly and is for a different list of 20 values. The number of comparisons should be approximately 40 for each of the three calls. Verify that the total, minimum, and maximum are correct for the reported number of comparisons.

Enter 10 for the array size. Enter 3 for the number of trials. Verify that each of the three sorts works correctly and is for a different list of 10 values. The number of comparisons should be approximately 13 for each of the three calls. Verify that the total, minimum, and maximum are correct for the reported number of comparisons

Step 5. Recomment the `print` statements from the previous step.

Final checkpoint: Compile and run the program. Enter 20 for the array size. Enter 10000 for the number of trials. The average should be within the range of 38 to 42 approximately 99% of the time.

Step 6. Fill in this table and the appropriate column in the table at the end of the directed lab. Use 100 trials.

Comparisons for Shell Sort

	MINIMUM COMPARISONS	AVERAGE COMPARISONS	MAXIMUM COMPARISONS
Size=10			
Size=50			
Size=100			
Size=200			
Size=300			
Size=400			
Size=500			
Size=750			
Size=1000			

Average Comparisons for All Three Sorts

	SELECTION SORT	INSERTION SORT	SHELL SORT
Size=10			
Size=50			
Size=100			
Size=200			
Size=300			
Size=400			
Size=500			
Size=750			
Size=1000			

Post-Lab Follow-Ups

1. Add a reset() method to SortArrayInstrumented that will set each of the variables as the constructor does. Modify SortDriver to compute the average, minimum, and maximum for each of the three sorts with the input array size and number of trials.

2. Add variables and methods to SortArrayInstrumented to compute the total of the squares of the number of comparisons. If the number of comparisons made by three calls were 3, 5, and 2, the sum of the squares would be 9 + 25 + 4. The variance of a list of values is the average of the squares of the values minus the square of the average. For the given values, the average is $10/3$ and the variance is $38/3-(10/3)^2$. The standard deviation is the square root of the variance. Use this to compute and display the standard deviation in SortDriver.

3. Another way of measuring the performance of a sort is by the amount of data movement it must do. Anytime an assignment is made using the array, add one to the number of moves. For example, a swap operation would add 3 to the number of moves. Add variables and methods to `SortArrayInstrumented` to compute the total, minimum, and maximum number of moves. Add code to `SortDriver` to display them.

   Note: This measure is relatively unimportant in Java since the sorts work with arrays of references to objects. Because of this, only references are being moved and not the objects themselves, and the time to complete the swap will not depend on the size of object.

4. Bubble sort is an older sort whose performance is not competitive with the other basic sorts. Outside of this exercise, you should not use bubble sort. One variant of bubble sort that works on the first n items in an array uses the following algorithm.

   > *First position is 0*
   > *Last position is n–2*
   > *While the first position is less than the last position*
   >   *Last swap is first position*
   >   *Loop i from first position to last position*
   >   *If elements at positions i and i+1 are out of order*
   >   *Swap the elements in positions i and i+1*
   >   *Last swap is i*
   >   *Last position is last swap*

   Implement and add statistics to bubble sort in `SortArrayInstrumented`. Compute the minimum, maximum, and average number of comparisons done by bubble sort.

5. The given Shell sort works with increments of 1, 2, 4, 8, ... (written in reverse order). The performance of Shell's sort can be improved by allowing more varied overlap between the sequences. Implement two new versions of Shell's sort that use the sequences.

   $$1, 4, 13, 40, 121 \qquad (s_i = 3s_{i-1} + 1)$$

   and

   $$1, 3, 7, 15, 31 \qquad (s_i = 2s_{i-1} + 1)$$

   Compute the minimum, maximum, and average number of comparisons done by these two versions of Shell's sort and compare with the original.

6. Generate $n\log_2 n$ random positions in the list that are at least $(\log_2 n)^2$ apart. If the items are out of order, switch them. Follow this by insertion sort. Compute the minimum, maximum and average number of comparisons done by this sort and compare with the standard insertion sort.

7. By counting the number of inversions in a list, you get a measure of how close the list is to being sorted. Consider every pair of values. (There are $n(n-1)/2$ pairs.) Each pair that is out of order contributes one to the number of inversions. Implement a method that counts the number of inversions in an array of `Comparable` objects.

8. While measuring the performance of a sort against randomly generated arrays is important, in real life data are often not random. Nearly sorted data are frequently encountered. Develop a method that generates random arrays that have at most k inversions. (Hint: Swapping two adjacent values adds at most one inversion.) Use this method to compute the performance of the three sorts for $k = n/2$, $k = n$, and $k = 2n$.

Lab 9　Advanced Sorts

Goal

In this lab you will explore the performance of quick sort and merge sort. The merge operation for merge sort will be modified. Partition from quick sort will be used in a new algorithm.

Resources

- Chapter 11: An Introduction to Sorting
- Chapter 12: Faster Sorting Methods
- *Lab9Graphs.pdf*—Printable versions of the graphs for this lab

Java Files

- *SortArray.java*
- *CheckSort.java*
- *CheckKth.java*
- *TimeSort.java*

Introduction

As mentioned in the first recursion lab, timing code introduces a number of difficulties. Unlike the number of comparisons, the time will vary from one test to the next. One reason for using timings instead of comparisons is that different versions of quick sort will be examined where factors besides the number of comparisons may affect the performance.

To make plotting the times easier, the ratio of the time with respect to quick sort on 100 values will be used.

Generic Recursive Sort

Both quick sort and merge sort are recursive algorithms and have essentially the same algorithm.

> Sort(L)
> 1. If small, just return L
> 2. Split L into L_1 and L_2
> 3. S_1 is Sort(L_1)
> 4. S_2 is Sort(L_2)
> 5. Return combine(S_1, S_2)

Merge sort does its work on the way up the recursion tree. Its split is easy. It divides the list in half. If merge sort is run in place on an array, the split operation consists of just computing the index of the middle. Combining the sorted lists, though, is where it does the work. The merge method will combine two sorted lists into one.

Quick sort, on the other hand, does its work on the way down the recursion tree. Its split is performed by the partition method, which will pick an element (pivot) in the list and then order the rest of the list with respect to it. The combination method for quick sort, on the other hand, is easy. The sorted lists just need to be spliced together. If quick sort is run in place on an array, the values are in their final positions already and the combine operation is "do nothing."

The split of quick sort depends on which data value is used as the pivot. Consequently, the performance of quick sort will vary depending on the order of values in the array to be sorted. Merge sort, on the other hand, will always split the list in half and is much less sensitive to the order of values in the array.

Variations of Quick Sort

The basic version of quick sort presented by most other textbooks has a partition method that chooses a fixed element as the pivot. Usually, either the first or last value in the range to be split is chosen. Quick sort then proceeds according to the general algorithm.

In practice, quick sort is the fastest general-purpose sort available, but there are a couple standard variations that improve the performance by a marginal amount.

The first improvement (version2QuickSort in the lab) is to notice that for small size lists, insertion sort is faster than quick sort. In part, the performance of quick sort is affected by the cost of doing a recursive call. An iterative insertion sort avoids this cost. Eventually, the increasing number of comparisons that insertion sort does will overtake the benefit of not doing the method calls. The improvement is to change the base case. For lists that are small, use an insertion sort. Instead of making a lot of calls to insertion sort, one single call after quick sort is finished will accomplish the same task.

The second improvement (version3QuickSort in the lab) is to choose a better pivot. The closer the split is to an even split, the better the performance of quick sort will be. Median-of-Three looks at three fixed values, usually the first, middle, and last elements. The values are ordered, and the middle value is chosen as the pivot. This has two benefits. The first benefit is that it is more likely that there will be a good split and the average performance is improved. Even so, a good split is not guaranteed and the worst case performance is still $O(n^2)$. The second benefit is that the worst case for the basic algorithm is on lists that are nearly sorted. Median-of-Three guarantees a good split on sorted data. Since nearly sorted data are fairly common, this shifts the worst case to orders that you expect to see less often.

Merge

The basic version of merge uses an extra array during merging. The following picture shows an intermediate state of the merge.

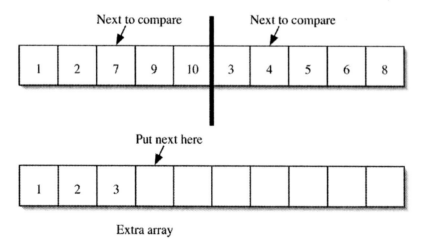

Extra array

Once all the values have been compared and placed in the extra array, the sorted values are copied back. Doing an in place merge that still has $O(n)$ behavior is a more challenging task.

Partition

Partition is a surprisingly tricky algorithm. The basic version used in the lab will pick the last value as the pivot. Two indices are used to scan the array. The first index scans the array from the left, looking for a value that is greater than the pivot. The second index scans the array from the right, looking for a value that is less than the pivot. (The pivot will be not scanned.) As long as the indices have not crossed over, the found values will be swapped.

Original

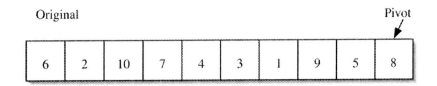

First swap to be made

Pivot

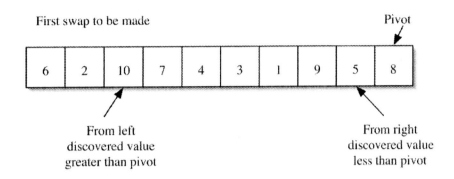

From left
discovered value
greater than pivot

From right
discovered value
less than pivot

Indices cross over

Pivot

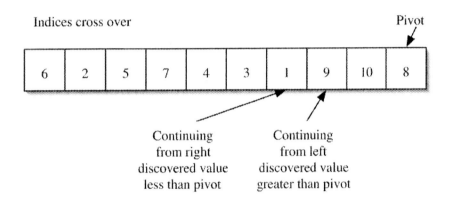

Continuing
from right
discovered value
less than pivot

Continuing
from left
discovered value
greater than pivot

Notice that all values from 9 on are greater than or equal to the pivot. All values left of the 9 are less than or equal to the pivot. The final step is to swap the pivot to split the partition.

Pivot is swapped to the correct position.

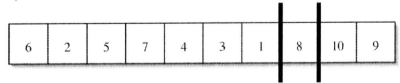

Partition with Median-of-Three

With Median-of-Three, partition first orders the values in the first, middle, and last positions.

Original

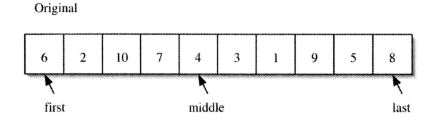

first   middle   last

Values are swapped
so they are ordered.

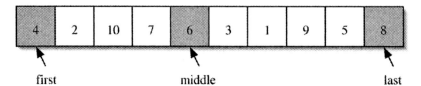

first   middle   last

Middle value is swapped with second to last.   pivot

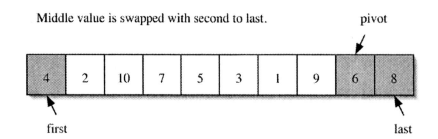

first   last

At this point, partition continues similarly to the basic version. Note that the first and last elements are guaranteed to be in the correct half of the partition.

First swap to be made   pivot

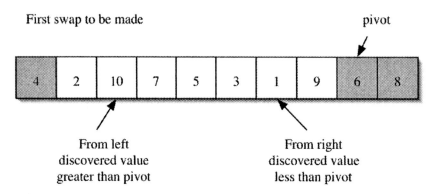

From left
discovered value
greater than pivot

From right
discovered value
less than pivot

Second swap to be made

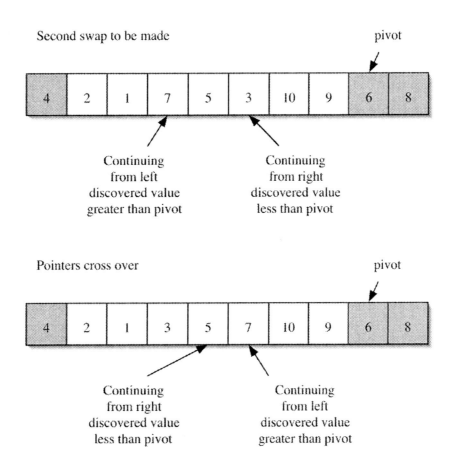

Continuing
from left
discovered value
greater than pivot

Continuing
from right
discovered value
less than pivot

Pointers cross over

Continuing
from right
discovered value
less than pivot

Continuing
from left
discovered value
greater than pivot

All values from 7 on are greater than or equal to the pivot. All values left of the 7 are less than or equal to the pivot. The final step is to swap the pivot to split the partition.

Pivot is swapped to the correct position.

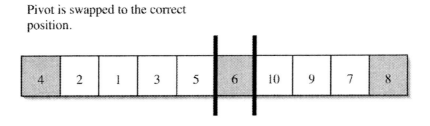

Pre-Lab Visualization

Bitonic Sequence

An in-place merge will be developed that will use the idea of a bitonic sequence. A bitonic sequence of values is one that can be divided into two parts. In one part, the values are increasing, and in the other part the values are decreasing.

For example, the following is a bitonic sequence.

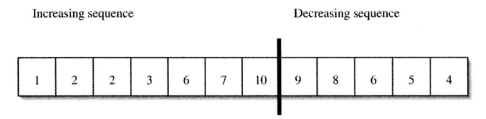

A sequence is also bitonic if it can be rotated and satisfy the preceding condition.

The following is, therefore, also a bitonic sequence.

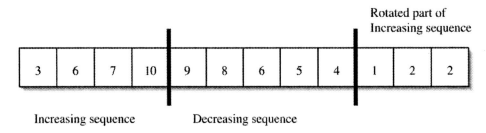

The following is a sequence that is not bitonic. No rotation can be found that will give just a single partition where the values are increasing.

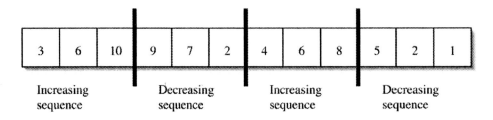

One final note: Either or both sequences can be empty. So the following sequence is bitonic.

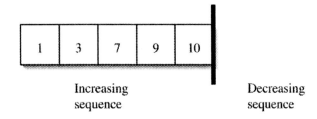

Bitonic Split

Given a bitonic sequence that has an even number of values, it can be split into two sequences. In the split operation, the list is divided into equal halves. The first values in each half are compared and, if out of order, they are swapped. Then the second values are compared, and so on until all values have been compared.

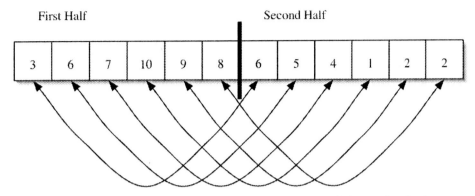

First Half   Second Half

| 3 | 6 | 7 | 10 | 9 | 8 | 6 | 5 | 4 | 1 | 2 | 2 |

What is the result after all pairs have been compared and swapped if out of order?

First half   Second half

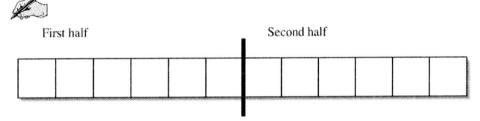

A bitonic split guarantees that all values in the first half are less than or equal to all values in the second half. Furthermore, it guarantees that each of the halves is a bitonic sequence.

What is the largest value in the first half?

What is the smallest value in the second half?

Give a rotation of the values in each half so that the values increase and then decrease.

First half   Second half

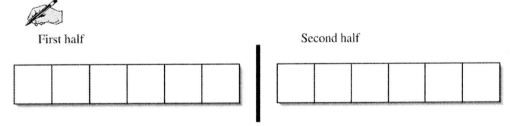

Give an algorithm for bitonic split.

Bitonic Merge

Given a bitonic sequence that has a number of values that is a power of 2, it can be merged into a single increasing sequence. As was seen, a bitonic split will result in a partition where all values in the first half are ordered with respect to all values in the second half. Since the resulting halves are also bitonic sequences, they each can be split. And then the quarters can be split, and so on.

Consider the following bitonic sequence of length 8.

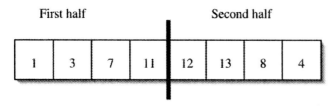

First half | Second half

| 1 | 3 | 7 | 11 | 12 | 13 | 8 | 4 |

What is the result after applying bitonic split?

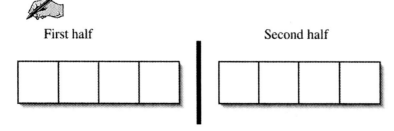

First half | Second half

What is the result after applying bitonic split to each of the halves?

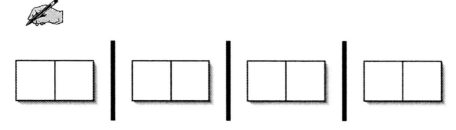

What is the result after applying bitonic split to each of the quarters?

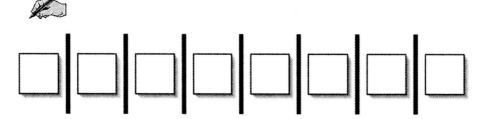

Suppose that there is a bitonic sequence which has $n = 2^k$ values. How many levels (splits of the same size) of bitonic splitting are needed?

In each level, how many comparisons are made?

What is the total number of comparisons made?

Give an algorithm for bitonic merge.

Bitonic Merge Sort

Given an appropriate bitonic sequence, it can be sorted using a bitonic merge. Think about the step just before merge does its combine. It has two portions of the array that are in increasing order. If one of the portions were reversed, the combination of the two portions would be a bitonic sequence. Then bitonic merge can be applied, resulting in a sorted array.

The advantage of the bitonic merge is that it can be done in place. Unfortunately, because the bitonic merge does not have linear time complexity, the bitonic merge sort is not $O(n \log_2 n)$ but instead is $O(n (\log_2 n)^2)$.

Order Statistics

Suppose there is a list of k values: $x_1, x_2, x_3, \ldots x_k$. One statistic that gives a measure of the central tendency of the values is called the median. If the values are sorted, the median is the middle value. Minimum and maximum are statistics that give the first and last values in the sorted list. Generalizing, the kth-order statistic is the kth value in the sorted list.

An obvious algorithm for finding the kth-order statistic for an array of values is:

kth(A, k)
      1.   Sort A
      2.   return the kth value in A

The performance of this algorithm will depend on the sort used. For quick sort, the average performance would be $O(n \log_2 n)$. It can be done faster, though.

Consider an array A containing the values 1, 2, …, 10.

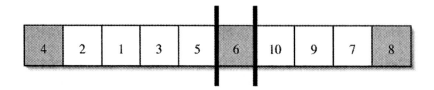

For this special array, the kth-order statistic is just the value k. After the array is sorted, at what location will the value k be found?

Consider the effects of partition. After partition is called, the array has been rearranged to:

| 4 | 2 | 1 | 3 | 5 | 6 | 10 | 9 | 7 | 8 |

If you were looking for the fourth-order statistic, in which part of the array will it be?

If you were looking for the sixth-order statistic, in which part of the array will it be?

If you were looking for the eighth-order statistic, in which part of the array will it be?

This suggests that a recursive auxiliary algorithm can be designed to find the kth-order statistic using partition.

Give a recursive design for the kth-order statistic.

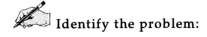 **Identify the problem:**

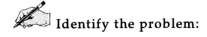 **Identify the smaller problems:**

 Identify how the answers are composed:

 Identify the base cases:

 Compose the recursive definition:

Trace the algorithm in finding the third-order statistic on the following array. (Show the result after each partition.) Once part of the array has been eliminated from consideration, just leave the values blank.

2	8	10	4	7	9	6	1	3	5

Directed Lab Work

The basic and advanced sorts have been implemented in the SortArray class. The class CheckSort will generate some arrays, call a sorting routine, and check that it correctly sorts the values. The class TimeSort will be used to time the sorts.

Deciding on Minimum Size

Step 1. If you have not done so, look at the implementation of the sorts in *SortArray.java*. Look at the code in *TimeSort.java*. Compile the classes SortArray and TimeSort.

Step 2. Run the main method in TimeSort. Enter 100 for the array size, 5000 for the number of trials, and 100 for the seed. Record the values in the following table. (If you get 0 for the quicksort time, redo with an increased number of trials.)

	TIME FOR BASIC QUICKSORT	TIME FOR INSERTION SORT	RATIO OF TIMES
Size=100			

Checkpoint: The actual values will depend on the platform. Quick sort should be fastest. Merge sort should be next fastest and roughly 1.7 times slower than basic quick sort. Insertion sort should be the slowest and be roughly 4 times slower than basic quick sort.

The first goal is to decide on an upper bound on the minimum size for arrays where quick sort should be invoked.

Step 3. Fill in the following table. Use 10000 for the number of trials and 100 for the seed.

	TIME FOR BASIC QUICKSORT	TIME FOR INSERTION SORT	RATIO OF TIMES
Size=2			
Size=4			
Size=6			
Size=8			
Size=10			
Size=12			
Size=14			
Size=16			
Size=18			
Size=20			

Step 4. It is expected that for small size lists, insertion sort will be faster than quick sort. Draw a line at the point where the ratio is 1 (i.e., the times are equal). (As mentioned in the Introduction, these times may not be consistent from execution to execution.)

You would expect that at the boundary where the times are equal, you could replace the recursive quick sort call with a call to insertion sort and the time would remain the same. In fact, the improved version of quick sort should be able to do better. Instead of calling insertion sort multiple times, it will wait until quick sort is finished and then make just a single call to insertion sort.

Step 5. Make a copy of timebasicQuickSort. Rename it to timeVersion2QuickSort. Change the call to version2QuickSort.

Step 6. Just after timing basicQuickSort, create a loop on minSize that runs from 2 to 20.

Step 7. Copy the nine lines that time merge sort into the body of the loop.

Step 8. Change the lines so that it reports for version 2 of quick sort.

Step 9. Add the following line at the beginning of the loop:

```
SortArray.setQuickSortMinimumSize(minSize);
```

Step 10. Add a line to print `minSize` in the loop.

Step 11. Fill in the following table. Use 1000 for the size of the list, 1000 for the number of trials, and 10 for the seed.

	TIME FOR VERSION 2 QUICKSORT	RATIO OF TIMES
minSize = 2		
minSize = 3		
minSize =4		
minSize = 5		
minSize = 6		
minSize = 7		
minSize = 8		
minSize = 9		
minSize = 10		
minSize = 11		
minSize = 12		
minSize = 13		
minSize = 14		
minSize = 15		
minSize = 16		
minSize = 17		
minSize = 18		
minSize = 19		
minSize = 20		

Step 12. Plot the ratios as points on the following graph.

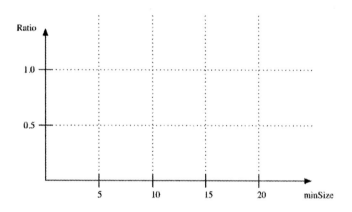

Step 13. Draw a curve approximating the points with a single minimum. It will look something like this:

Step 14. Choose a value that is close to the minimum of the curve. It should be less than the upper bound that was found earlier. Record that value here.

Timing the Sorts

Step 15. Comment out the `for` loop you added to `main` of `TimeSort`.

Step 16. Make a copy of `timeVersion2QuickSort`. Change the name to `timeVersion3QuickSort`. Change it so it calls `version3QuickSort()`.

Step 17. Make two copies of the lines in `main` that time merge sort.

Step 18. Change the first copy to use version 2 quick sort instead of merge sort.

Step 19. Change the second copy to use version 3 quick sort instead of merge sort.

Step 20. Add a call to `setQuickSortMinimumSize` just before the two copies. Use the value you recorded at the end of the previous section as the argument.

Because different machines will have different performance, the absolute time will not be used. Instead the ratio of the time with respect to basic quick sort on an array of size 100 will be used.

Step 21. Create a new variable of type `double` named `quickSort100Time` and assign it the value
`trials * ##### * 1000`,
where ##### is the value you recorded for the time of quick sort in the first table.

Step 22. Copy the print statement for the ratio from the merge sort section to section for basic quick sort.

Step 23. Change the print statement so it uses `quickSortTime` instead of `mergeSortTime`.

Step 24. In all of the print statements that compute a ratio, change them so that they use `quickSort100Time` in the denominator. (There should be five in all.)

Step 25. Run the program with 1000 for the size, 1 for the number of trials, and 10 for the initial seed. Note the time for computing the insertion sort. For the following table, pick the number of trials so that the total insertion sort computation time is at least 1 minute.

 Trials:

Step 26. Fill in the following table. Use the number of trials you computed in the previous step. Use 10 for the seed.

	RATIO FOR BASIC QUICKSORT	RATIO FOR QUICK SORT II	RATIO FOR QUICK SORT III	RATIO FOR MERGE SORT	RATIO FOR INSERTION SORT
Size=100					
Size=200					
Size=300					
Size=400					
Size=500					
Size=600					
Size=700					
Size=800					
Size=900					
Size=1000					

Step 27. Plot the points for the ratios for the three quick sort versions and merge sort in the following graph. (Use different colors for the points.) Draw smooth curves approximating the points.

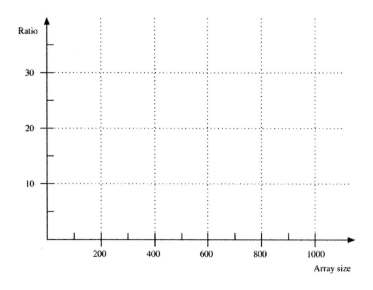

Step 28. Plot the points for the ratios for basic quick sort, merge sort, and insertions sort in the following graph. Draw smooth curves approximating the points.

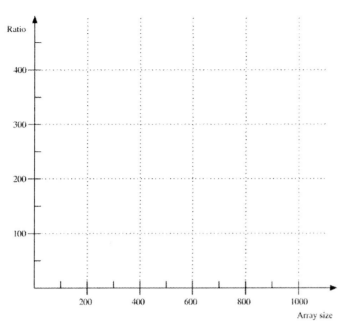

Step 29. Use the value of the ratio for basic quick sort with an array size of 500 (n=500) to solve the equation:

$$\text{ratio} = k_{\text{quick}} \, n \log_2 n$$

for k_{quick}.

Step 30. Use the value of the ratio for merge sort with an array size of 500 to solve the equation:

$$\text{ratio} = k_{\text{merge}} \, n \log_2 n$$

for k_{merge}.

Step 31. Plot the points for the ratios for basic quick and merge sort on the following graph.

Step 32. Draw the curves:

$$k_{quick} \, n \log_2 n$$

and

$$k_{merge} \, n \log_2 n$$

for the computed values of k_{quick} and k_{merge}.

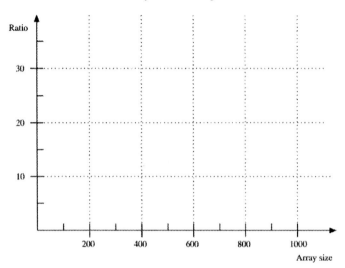

Step 33. Use the value of the ratio for insertion sort with an array size of 500 to solve the equation

$$\text{ratio} = k_{insertion} \, n^2$$

for $k_{insertion}$. (n=500)

Step 34. Plot the points for the ratios of insertion sort on the following graph.

Step 35. Draw the curve:

$$k_{insertion} \, n^2$$

for the computed value of $k_{insertion}$.

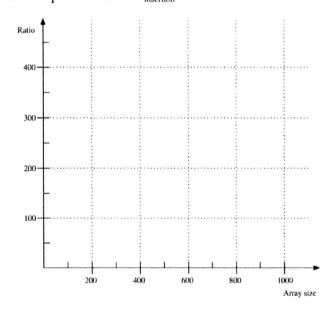

Bitonic Merge

Step 1.   In SortArray make a copy of the code for merge sort.

Step 2.   In the copy, change merge to bitonicMerge.

Step 3.   Comment out the code from the body of the bitonic merge.

Step 4.   Add code that does a bitonic split on the whole bitonic sequence (the first half in sorted order combined with the second half in reverse sorted order.) Refer to the Pre-Lab.

Step 5.   Finish the code for bitonic merge so that it will do the appropriate bitonic spilt operations on smaller and smaller sections of the array. This can be done either iteratively or recursively.

Step 6.   Add code in bitonicMergeSort before the call to bitonicMerge that will reverse the second half.

Step 7.   In CheckSort, change the call from insertionSort to bitonicMergeSort.

Checkpoint: Run CheckSort with an array size of 512. Verify that bitonic merge sort works correctly. If it fails, debugging with array sizes that are small (like 2, 4, and 8) may be helpful. Remember that the array size must be a power of 2.

Step 8.   Make a copy of timeMergeSort().

Step 9.   Change the name to timeBitonicMergeSort.

Step 10.   Modify it to time the bitonic merge sort.

Step 11.   Make a copy of the nine lines in main that time merge sort.

Step 12.   Make the copy time bitonic merge sort.

Step 13.   Comment out the code that times insertion sort and versions 2 and 3 of quick sort.

Fill in the following table. Use the number of trials you computed for the previous section. Use 10 for the seed.

	RATIO FOR BASIC QUICKSORT	RATIO FOR MERGE SORT	RATIO FOR BITONIC MERGE SORT
Size=128			
Size=256			
Size=512			
Size=1024			
Size=2048			

Step 14. Use the value of the ratio for bitonic merge sort with an array size of 512 to solve the equation

$$\text{ratio} = k_{bitonic}\, n\, (\log_2 n)^2$$

for $k_{bitonic}$.

Step 15. Plot the points for the ratios for merge sort and bitonic merge sort on the following graph.

Step 16. Draw the curves

$k_{merge}\, n \log_2 n$

and

$k_{bitonic}\, n\, (\log_2 n)^2$
for the computed values of k_{merge} and $k_{bitonic}$.

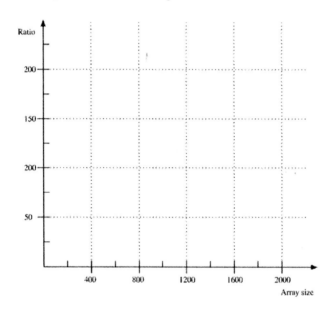

Order Statistics

Step 17. In SortArray look at the existing code for kthItem(). The private recursive method needs to be completed.

Step 18. Refer the algorithm from the Pre-Lab Exercises and complete the kthItem() method.

Checkpoint: Run CheckKth with an array size of 10. If it passes, run it again with an array size of 1000. If it fails, debug and retest.

Step 19. Make a copy of timeQuickSort().

Step 20. Change the name to timeKth().

Step 21. Modify it to time kthItem(). Always have it get the smallest item (k=1).

Step 22. Make a copy of the nine lines in main that time merge sorts.

Step 23. Make the copy use timeKth().

Step 24. Fill in the following table. Use the number of trials you computed for the previous section. Use 10 for the seed.

	RATIO FOR BASIC QUICKSORT	RATIO FOR K-TH ITEM
Size=100		
Size=200		
Size=300		
Size=400		
Size=500		
Size=600		
Size=700		
Size=800		
Size=900		
Size=1000		

Step 25. Use the value of the ratio for `kthItem()` item with an array size of 500 to solve the equation

$$\text{ratio} = k_{kth} \, n$$

for k_{kth}.

Step 26. Plot the points for the ratios for basic quick sort and `kthItem()` on the following graph.

Step 27. Draw the curves

$$k_{quick} \, n \log_2 n$$

and

$$k_{kth} \, n$$

for the computed values of k_{quick} and k_{kth}.

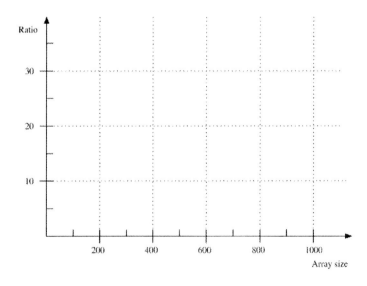

Post-Lab Follow-Ups

1. Create a method checkPowerOf2(int n) that returns true if n is a power of 2. Use this method in the public version of bitonicMergeSort to throw an exception if the argument n is not a power of 2.

2. Create a new version of bitonic merge that will work with an odd number of values. **Hint**: Compare values as before. The extra value is at the end of the first list. Decide if it must be in the first or second half and adjust the subsequent bitonic splits appropriately. Use CheckSort to verify that the new code works correctly. Redo the timing with the new version and compare with the original.

3. Create two versions of bitonic merge sort: bitonicMergeSortAscending and bitonicMergeSortDescending. Remove the call to reverse and replace the recursive calls to bitonicMergeSort with the two new methods. Use CheckSort to verify that the new code works correctly. Redo the timing with the new version and compare with the original.

4. Replace the iterative version of bitonicMerge with a recursive version (or vice-verse if you implemented a recursive bitonic merge.) Use CheckSort to verify that the new code works correctly. Redo the timing with the new version and compare with the original.

5. Implement kthItem using basicPartition. Use CheckKth to verify that the new code works correctly. Redo the timing with the new version and compare with the original. Explain the results.

6. Implement an iterative version of kthItem. Use CheckKth to verify that the new code works correctly. Redo the timing with the new version and compare with the original.

7. Create a second random number generator and change timeKthItem() to look for a random position in the sorted list. Compare the times with searching for the smallest item (first position).

Lab 10   Searches

Goal

In this lab you will explore the performance of various searches. You will implement new searches including an alternate version of binary search and a trinary search. You will modify the searches to work with the List API from Java.

Resources

- Chapter 16: Searching
- *java.sun.com/j2se/1.5.0/docs/api*—API documentation for the Java List interface
- *Lab10Graphs.pdf*—Printable versions of the graphs for this lab

Java Files

- *SortArray.java*
- *CheckSearch.java*
- *TimeSearch.java*
- *CheckSortList.java*
- *CheckSearchList.java*

Introduction

One reason many lists are sorted is to improve the performance of searching. Linear search has performance that, on average, is O(n) in the size of the list. Binary search will work in time that is O(log$_2$ n), but it requires that the list is sorted.

Suppose you wanted to search a list for just a single data value? Which would be faster, linear search or binary search? The answer depends on the data. If the data are already sorted, binary search wins. On the other hand, if the data are unsorted, the cost of the binary search must include the sort and plain linear search wins.

Consider what happens if you need to search for more than one data value. The linear search has no initial cost, but each subsequent search costs O(n). The binary search has an initial cost of O(n log$_2$ n) for the sort, but each subsequent search only costs O(log$_2$ n). If the number of searches is large enough, binary search will win.

Another way of viewing this is that the O(n log$_2$ n) cost of the sort is spread out over k searches. Therefore, the per search cost for binary sort is O((n/k) log$_2$ n + log$_2$ n).

Pre-Lab Visualization

Splitting a Range in an Array

As with the other recursive algorithms that work on an array, binary search works with a range of values. When an algorithm of this type fails, it is usually for a small range.

In the standard version of binary search, the formula for computing the index of the middle value is

$$middle = (first + last)/2\,.$$

Consider the following range of values:

INDEX	...	3	4	...
VALUE		20	40	

What is the index of the middle?

There are three cases that will be considered depending on the relation between the middle value and the value that is being searched for.

The middle value is greater than the values being searched for.
In this case, the value that is being searched for must be to the left of the middle. Make a recursive call to the range first to mid–1. In the preceding example, if the desired value was 10, what is the next search range?

The middle value is the value being searched for.
In this case, no more work is needed, just return true.

The middle value is less than the value being searched for.
In this case, the value that is being searched for must be to the right of the middle. Make a recursive call to the range mid+1 to last. In the preceding example, if the desired value was 45, what is the next search range?

Notice that it is possible for the range to become empty.

This style of splitting for binary search has an early exit feature. As the array is probed, if the value is found, stop the recursion and return.

Binary Search in an Array with Late Checking
Suppose there is an array with n values.

How many of those values, if searched for, will have an early exit at the first split?

How many of those values, if searched for, will have an early exit at the second split?

How many of those values, if searched for, will have an early exit at the third split?

How many of those values, if searched for, will have an early exit at the final split?

Look at the code for binary search in SortArray and notice that there are potentially two comparisons made. One by equals() and the other by compareTo(). Most of the values in the array will not benefit from early exit and will need close to $2 \log_2 n$ comparisons. If the value being searched for is not in the array, no early exit can take place.

There is another version of binary search that only does one comparison per recursive call. The range is reduced until there is just a single value left. That value is then compared to the desired value.

To handle this, splitting the range must change.

There are still three cases, but two of them will be handled together.

The middle value is greater than the values being searched for.
In this case, the value that is being searched for must be to the left of the middle. What should the range be for the next search?

The middle value is the value being searched for.
We need to guarantee that the next search range will contain the middle value. What should the range be for the next search?

The middle value is less than the value being searched for.
In this case, the value that is being searched for must be to the right of the middle. What should the range be for the next search?

Which two cases use the same range?

This time, the range should not become empty but will reduce to a single value. This affects the base case.

Complete the design for late check binary search on an array. Use a recursive auxiliary method that reduces the range of values considered. Make sure that each recursive call will do either equals() or compareTo(), but not both.

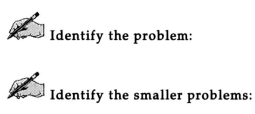 Identify the problem:

 Identify the smaller problems:

 Identify how the answers are composed:

 Identify the base cases:

 Compose the recursive definition:

Show the operation of your definition when searching for the value 3 in the array [2 4 5 6 7 9].

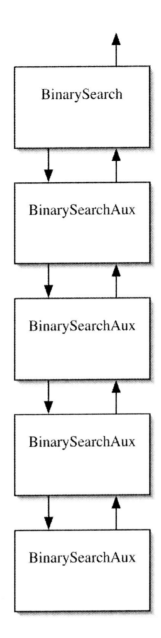

Trinary Search in an Array

Another way that you might try to speed up binary search is to split the array into three parts instead of two.

Given that *first* and *last* are the indices of the range of values to consider, propose formulas that will compute two middle values that trisect the range.

 *middle1* =

 *middle2* =

Test these formulas on each of the following small ranges.

For each of the following range of values, compute middle1 and middle2.

INDEX	...	4	....
VALUE		40	

 *middle1 =*

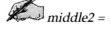 *middle2 =*

INDEX	...	3	4	....
VALUE		20	40	

 *middle1 =*

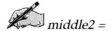 *middle2 =*

INDEX	...	3	4	5	...
VALUE		20	40	60	

 *middle1 =*

 middle2 =

INDEX	...	4	5	6	7	...
VALUE		40	60	90	110	

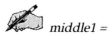 *middle1 =*

 middle2 =

Are middle1 and middle2 always different?

The trinary search can either use either strategy of early exit or late checking for equality. In either case, there are now five cases that must be considered.

The value being searched for is less than middle1.
What should the range be for the next search?

The value being searched for is equal to middle1.
What should the range be for the next search?

The value being searched for is greater than middle1 and less than middle2.
What should the range be for the next search?

The value being searched for is equal to middle2.
What should the range be for the next search?

The value being searched for is greater than middle2.
What should the range be for the next search?

Think about what happens to the splits for small ranges. Can there be empty ranges?

Complete the design for trinary search on an array. Use a recursive auxiliary method that reduces the range of values considered.

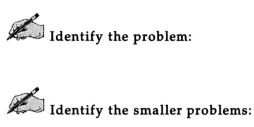 Identify the problem:

Identify the smaller problems:

Identify how the answers are composed:

Identify the base cases:

Compose the recursive definition:

Show the operation of your definition when searching for the values 3, 5, 6, and 10 in the array [2 4 5 6 7 9]. (Depending on the actual algorithm, less than three recursive calls maybe needed. If so, just cross off the extra boxes in the diagram.)

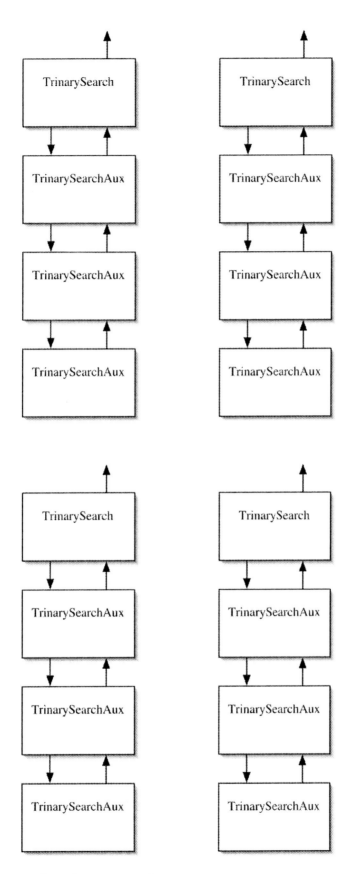

These are not exhaustive test cases by any means.

Directed Lab Work

Linear and binary search have been implemented in the SortArray class. The class CheckSearch will generate some arrays, call a search routine, and check that it correctly searches for values. It guarantees that some values not in the array are searched for. The class TimeSearch will be used to time the searches.

Timing the Searches

Step 1. If you have not done so, look at the implementation of the search routines in *SortArray.java*. Look at the code in *TimeSearch.java*. Compile the classes SortArray and TimeSearch.

Step 2. Run the main method in TimeSort. Enter 100 for the array size, 10000 for the number of trials, 1 for the number of searches, and 100 for the seed. Record the time in the following table.

	TIME FOR VERSION 3 QUICKSORT
Size=100	

Step 3. In the definition of quickSort100Time, replace 6e-4 with the value you found in the previous step.

Step 4. Run the main method in TimeSort. Enter 100 for the array size, 10000 for the number of trials, 1 for the number of searches, and 100 for the seed. Record the values in the following tables.

	TIME FOR LINEAR SEARCH
Size=100	

	RATIO FOR QUICKSORT	RATIO FOR LINEAR SEARCH	RATIO FOR A SINGLE SORT THEN BINARY SEARCH	RATIO FOR SORT THEN BINARY SEARCH
Size=100				

Checkpoint: The actual values will depend on the platform. The ratio for quick sort should be about 1. Linear search should have a ratio that is about 0.1. Since only one search is being performed on each array, both binary searches should have a time that is approximately 1. In this case, the major cost for the binary searches is the sort.

Step 5. Run the main method in TimeSort. Enter 100 for the array size, 10000 for the number of trials, 10 for the number of searches, and 100 for the seed. Record the values in the following table.

	RATIO FOR QUICKSORT	RATIO FOR LINEAR SEARCH	RATIO FOR A SINGLE SORT THEN BINARY SEARCH	RATIO FOR SORT THEN BINARY SEARCH
Size=100				

Checkpoint: The values should be about the same as before with the exception of the single sort followed by binary searches, which should be about 0.1. The cost of the single sort has been divided between the 10 searches.

The first goal is to complete timings for linear and binary search. Since it has been established that sorting the array each time before doing the binary search has performance that is essentially the same as doing the sort, it will be dropped from timing. To reduce the effect of the sort required for *binary search, a large number of searches will be done. Note that the leading term in the time for doing a single sort followed by multiple binary searches will still be nlogn. If n is large compared to the number of searches the sorting time will dominate.*

Step 6. Comment out the code for timing quick sort.

Step 7. Comment out the code for timing sort followed by binary search.

Step 8. Take 6 seconds and divide it by the time recorded for linear search on an array of size 100 and record it here.

S= NUMBER OF SEARCHES TO DO	

Step 9. Fill in the following table. Use 1 for number of trials, S for the number of searches, and 100 for the seed.

	RATIO FOR LINEAR SEARCH	RATIO FOR BINARY SEARCH
Size=100		
Size=200		
Size=300		
Size=400		
Size=500		
Size=600		
Size=700		
Size=800		
Size=900		
Size=1000		

Step 10. Use the value of the ratio for linear search with an array size of 500 (n=500) to solve the equation:
$$\text{ratio} = k_{linear} \, n$$

for k_{linear}.

Step 11. Use the value of the ratio for binary search with an array size of 500 to solve the equation:
$$\text{ratio} = k_{binary} \, \log_2 n$$

for k_{binary}.

Step 12. Plot the points for the ratios for linear and binary search on the following graph.

Step 13. Draw the curves:

$$k_{linear} \, n$$

and

$$k_{binary} \, \log_2 n$$

for the computed values of k_{linear} and k_{binary}.

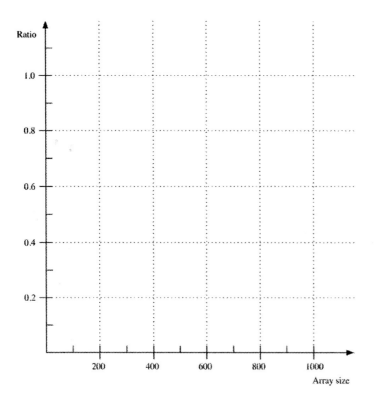

As seen earlier, for a small number of searches linear search is faster than sorting followed by doing binary search. The next goal is to determine at what point it is faster to do the binary search.

Step 14. Fill in the following table. For each given size, find the number of searches where the times for linear and binary searches become the same. Use 100 for the number of trials and 100 for the seed. You may wish to add loops to TimeSearch to automate its generation.

	NUMBER OF SEARCHES AT WHICH THE TIME FOR LINEAR AND BINARY SEARCH IS THE SAME
Size=100	
Size=200	
Size=300	
Size=400	
Size=500	
Size=600	
Size=700	
Size=800	
Size=900	
Size=1000	

Step 15. Plot the points for the number of searches required for linear and binary search to take the same amount of time on the following graph.

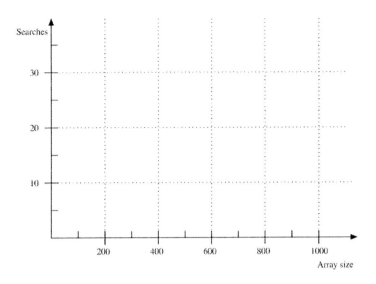

Step 16. Which of the following best fits the points? (Solve for k at 500 and then sketch the curve.)

k n

k $\log_2$ n

k $n^{0.5}$

k n $\log_2$ n

k n^2

Alternate Version of Binary Search

As discussed earlier, the version of binary search implemented in SortArray checks for equality on each recursive call. If it finds the value, it exits early and ends the recursion. The goal is to complete and time the new version of binary search.

Step 17. In SortArray, make a copy of the two methods named binarySearch() that implement binary search.

Step 18. In the copy, change binarySearch to version2BinarySearch everywhere.

Step 19. Change the private method version2BinarySearch so that it does not exit the recursion early, but only checks for equality at the very last recursive call. Refer to the Pre-Lab Exercises.

Step 20. In CheckSearch, change the call from binarySearch to version2BinarySearch.

Checkpoint: Run CheckSearch with an array size of 10, number of trials of 10, and a seed of 10. Verify that the new version of binary search works correctly. If it fails, debugging with array sizes that are small may be helpful.

Run CheckSearch with an array size of 1000, number of trials of 1, and a seed of 10. Verify that the new version of binary search works correctly.

Step 21. Make a copy of timeSingleSortAndBinarySearch().

Step 22. Change the name to `timeSingleSortAndVersion2BinarySearch`.

Step 23. Modify it to time version 2 binary search.

Step 24. Make a copy of the nine lines in `main` that time a single sort and binary search.

Step 25. Make the copy time `timeSingleSortAndVersion2BinarySearch`.

Step 26. Fill in the following table. Use 1 for number of trials, S (from Step 8) for the number of searches, and 100 for the seed.

	RATIO FOR BINARY SEARCH	RATIO FOR VERSION 2 OF BINARY SEARCH
Size=100		
Size=200		
Size=300		
Size=400		
Size=500		
Size=600		
Size=700		
Size=800		
Size=900		
Size=1000		

Trinary Search

The goal is to implement a search that splits the list into three parts instead of just two parts. Once the search works, it will be timed and the performance will be compared with binary search.

Step 1. In `SortArray` make a copy of the two methods named `binarySearch()` that implement binary search.

Step 2. In the copy, change `binarySearch` to `trinarySearch` everywhere.

Step 3. Change the private method `trinarySearch` so that it does a trinary search. Refer to the Pre-Lab Exercises.

Step 4. In `CheckSearch`, change the call from `version2BinarySearch` to `trinarySearch`.

Checkpoint: Run CheckSort with an array size of 10, number of trials of 10, and a seed of 10. Verify that trinary search works correctly. If it fails, debugging with array sizes that are small may be helpful.

Run CheckSort with an array size of 1000, number of trials of 1, and a seed of 10. Verify that trinary search works correctly.

Step 5. Make a copy of `timeSingleSortAndBinarySearch()`.

Step 6. Change the name to `timeSingleSortAndTrinarySearch`.

Step 7. Modify it to time trinary search.

Step 8. Make a copy of the nine lines in `main` that time a single sort and binary search.

Step 9. Make the copy time `timeSingleSortAndTrinarySearch`.

Step 10. Fill in the following table. Use 1 for number of trials, S (from Step 8) for the number of searches, and 100 for the seed.

	RATIO FOR BINARY SEARCH	RATIO FOR TRINARY SEARCH
Size=100		
Size=200		
Size=300		
Size=400		
Size=500		
Size=600		
Size=700		
Size=800		
Size=900		
Size=1000		

Step 11.   Use the value of the ratio for trinary search with an array size of 500 to solve the equation

$$\text{ratio} = k_{\text{trinary}} \log_3 n$$

for k_{trinary}.

Step 12.   Plot the points for the ratios for binary and trinary search on the following graph.

Step 13.   Draw the curves

$$k_{\text{binary}} \log_2 n$$

and

$$k_{\text{trinary}} \log_3 n$$

for the computed values of k_{binary} and k_{trinary}.

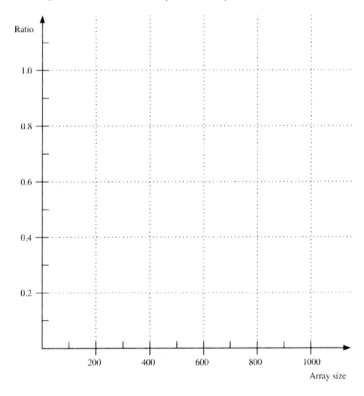

Step 14. Now use the value of the ratio for trinary search with an array size of 500 to solve the equation:

$$ratio = K \log_2 n$$

for K (Note that the base of the log is different from the base used in Step 11).

Step 15. Draw the curve:

$$K \log_2 n$$

for the computed value of K on the previous graph.

Step 16. What can you conclude about the order of growth of trinary search as compared with the order of growth for binary search?

Search on a List

Step 17. Make a new class named `SortList`.

Step 18. Copy all the code from `SortArray` to `SortList`.

Step 19. Remove all of the code except for the methods that perform swap, insertion sort, quick sort version 3, sort first middle last, order, partition, linear search, and binary search.

Step 20. Import the `java.util` package by adding the following statement at the top of the file.
```
import java.util.*;
```

Step 21. Replace all of the `T[]` declarations with `List<T>`. (Anything that is just T, leave as is.)

Step 22. Everywhere except on the left-hand side of an assignment statement, replace:

```
a[i]
```
with
```
a.get(i)
```

Step 23. For occurences of a[i] on the left-hand side of assignment statements, replace:

```
a[i] = x;
```

with

```
a.set(i, x);
```

Checkpoint: SortList should now compile.

Verify that version 3 quick sort works by running CheckSortList. Use 10 lists of size 10. If it passes, try again with a single list of size 1000. If it fails, debug and retest.

Verify that linear and binary searches work by running CheckSearchList. Use 10 lists of size 10. If it passes, try again with a single list of size 1000. If it fails, debug and retest.

Step 24. Make a new class named `TimeSearchList`.

Step 25. Copy all the code from `TimeSearch` to `TimeSearchList`.

Step 26. Remove the methods `timeSortAndBinarySearch()`, `timeSingleSortAndTrinarySearch()`, and `timeSingleSortAndVersion2BinarySearch()`.

Step 27. Look at the code in the method `timeArrayCreation()`. Replace it with code that will generate a `List<Integer>` instead of an array. Generate the same data values. Examine the method `generateRandomList()` in `CheckSortList` to see an example. Use `ArrayList<Integer>` as the type of the list that is created. Make a similar change in the other timing methods.

Step 28. Fill in the first two columns of the following table. Use 1 for number of trials, S/2 for the number of searches, and 100 for the seed.

Step 29. Change the code in `TimeSearchList` to create `LinkedList<Integer>` instead of `ArrayList<Integer>`.

Step 30. Fill in the last two columns of the table. Use 1 for number of trials, S/20 for the number of searches, and 100 for the seed.

	RATIO FOR LINEAR SEARCH (ARRAY LIST)	RATIO FOR BINARY SEARCH (ARRAY LIST)	RATIO FOR LINEAR SEARCH (LINKED LIST)	RATIO FOR BINARY SEARCH (LINKED LIST)
Size=100				
Size=200				
Size=300				
Size=400				
Size=500				
Size=600				
Size=700				
Size=800				
Size=900				
Size=1000				

Step 31. Compare the ratios for linear search on an array list and on a linked list. What is the relationship between the results?

Step 32. Do the ratios for binary search on an array list and on a linked list satisfy the same relationship that you found in the previous step?

Step 33. Plot the points for the ratios for linear search on an array list and linked list on the following graph.

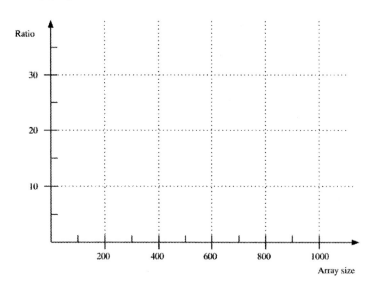

Step 34. Which of the following best fits the points for the linked list?

k n

k $\log_2$ n

k $n^{0.5}$

k n $\log_2$ n

k n^2

Step 35. Plot just the points for the ratio for linear search on an array list on the following graph.

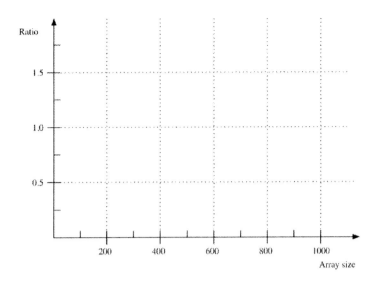

Step 36. Which of the following best fits the points for the array list?

k n

k log$_2$ n

k n$^{0.5}$

k n log$_2$ n

k n^2

Step 37. Plot the points for the ratios for binary search on an array list and linked list on the following graph.

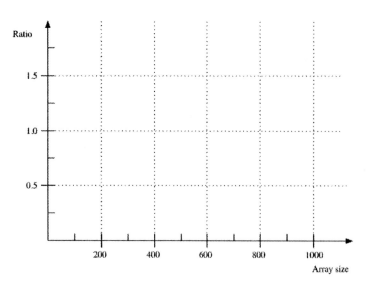

Step 38. Which of the following best fits the points for the linked list?

k n

k $\log_2$ n

k $n^{0.5}$

k n $\log_2$ n

k n^2

Step 39.   Plot just the points for the ratio for binary search on an array list on the following graph.

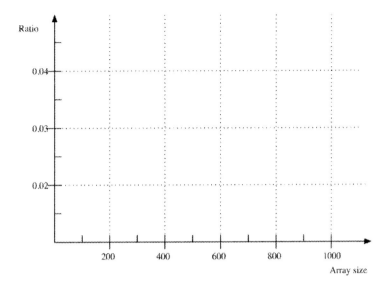

Step 40.   Which of the following best fits the points for the array list?

k n

k log$_2$ n

k n$^{0.5}$

k n log$_2$ n

k n^2

Step 41.   Explain the results found in the previous four graphs.

Post-Lab Follow-Ups

1. Suppose the time to do k searches on an array of size n is $n\log_2 n + k\log_2 n$. How large must n be before the sorting time (first term) is larger than the searching time (second term)?

2. Create an iterative version of `binarySearch`. Use `CheckSearch` to verify that the new code works correctly. Redo the timing with the new version and compare with the original.

3. Modify the recursive binary search so it only calls `compareTo()` once but still has early exit of the recursion. Compare the timing with the original.

4. Develop and implement the other version of trinary search. If you did early exit trinary search in the lab, implement trinary search with late checking.

5. Develop and implement a recursive search routine that uses a similar pattern to the kth-order statistics from the last lab. Compare the performance with linear search.

6. Develop and implement a recursive search routine based on binary search that works with numerical data. Assume that the data are evenly distributed. Use the values of the first and last data items to decide where to split the list. This is similar to how most people search a phone book. If you are looking for a name starting with the letter z, the first split will be toward the end, whereas if the name starts with the letter a, the first split will be toward the beginning. For example, suppose the value being searched for was 7. If the first value is 2 at location 3 and the last value is 100 at location 20, then the split would be at the index $3+ [(7-2)/(100-2)](20-3)$. Compare the performance with linear search.

7. Compare the ratios for quick sort on an array, `ArrayList`, and `LinkedList`. Determine the order of growth for each. Implement selection sort and merge sort on a `List`. Do timings and compare with the versions that work with an array.

8. Change the linear search in `SortList` so that it uses an iterator instead of the `get()` method. Compare the performance with the original version. Can an iterator be used to speed up binary search?

Lab 11   Dictionary Client

Goal

In this lab you will use a dictionary in an animated application to highlight words that could be misspelled in a text file.

Resources

- Chapter 17: Dictionaries
- Appendix C: File Input and Output
- *DictionaryInterface.html*—API documentation for the DictionaryInterface ADT
- *Wordlet.html*—API documentation for a class representing a word with a flag for whether it is spelled correctly
- *LinesToDisplay.html*—API documentation for a class representing a number of lines to be displayed graphically
- *java.sun.com/j2se/1.5.0/docs/api*—API documentation for the Scanner class
- *java.sun.com/j2se/1.5.0/docs/api*—API documentation for the StringTokenizer class
- *Spell.jar*—The final animated application

Java Files

In directory *Spelling Checker*
- *FindDefaultDirectory.java*
- *Wordlet.java*
- *LinesToDisplay.java*
- *MisspellActionThread.java*
- *MisspellApplication.java*
- *HashedMapAdaptorr.java*—in the DictionaryPackage
- There are other files used to animate the application. For a full description see Appendix A.

Input Files

- *check.txt*—A short text file to check for possible spelling errors
- *sampleDictionary.txt*—A small dictionary

Introduction

The dictionary ADT is set of associations between two items: the key and the value. A concrete example is a dictionary, such as the *Oxford English Dictionary*. It associates words with their definitions. Given a key (word), you can find its value (definition).

There are a number of ways you could implement the dictionary ADT. In this lab a hash table will be used to implement the dictionary. The details of how hash tables work will be considered in depth later (Chapter 19). For now, the important features of a hash table are that they allow fast access and that the items in the hash table are not ordered by their keys.

Pre-Lab Visualization

Loading the Dictionary

Given a dictionary of words and a word to be checked for spelling, what is the key? (What is being searched for?)

Reading the file that contains correctly spelled words into the dictionary requires that the file must be parsed (the file must be broken up into pieces each containing a single word). Sometimes the format of the file will be tightly specified. In this case, the format will be pretty loose. The correct words will be in a file. They will be separated by either space or return. Review Appendix C of the text and the API for Scanner.

Write an algorithm for reading the words from a file. Assume that the file is already opened as an instance of Scanner with the name input.

Wordlet Class

As the spelling checker executes, it will need to consider each word in the text. As it decides whether a word is spelled correctly or not, that information will need to be associated with the word. The function of the Wordlet class is to remember whether the word is spelled correctly.

The Wordlet class holds a chunk of text and a boolean variable indicating if the word is spelled correctly. Review that class if you have not done so already.

LinesToDisplay Class

A data structure is needed to hold the lines of wordlets that will be displayed by the animated application. Here are the requirements for the class.

1. It must contain up to 10 lines of checked text.
2. It must know whether words are spelled correctly.
3. It must have a line of text that it is currently composing.
4. It must be able to add a wordlet to the current line.
5. It must be able to move to the next line of text.

Consider the wordlets in a single line. Would an array or a list be preferable for storing them?

Suppose that the initial state is

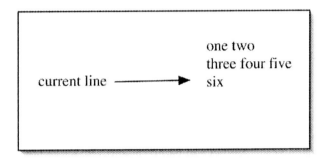

Show the new state if the wordlet " " (a single blank) is added.

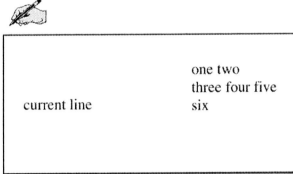

What should be displayed in the animation?

Show the new state if the wordlet "seven" is added instead.

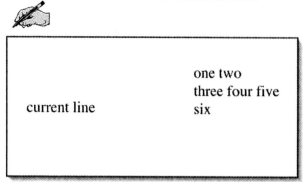

one two
three four five
six

current line

What should be displayed in the animation?

Show the new state if the current line is ended.

one two
three four five
six

current line

What should be displayed in the animation?

Suppose that the initial state is:

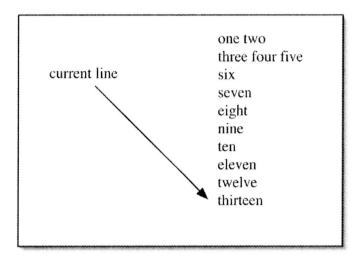

Show the new state if the line is ended and then the wordlet "fourteen" is added.

one two
three four five
current line   six
seven
eight
nine
ten
eleven
twelve
thirteen

Are there more than ten lines of text to be displayed?

What should be displayed in the animation?

Show the new state if the line is ended and then the wordlet "fifteen" is added.

```
                        one two
                        three four five
        current line    six
                        seven
                        eight
                        nine
                        ten
                        eleven
                        twelve
                        thirteen
```

Are there more than ten lines of text to be displayed?

What should be displayed in the animation?

Given that the private state variables of the class are

```
public static final int LINES = 10; // Display 10 lines
private ArrayList<Wordlet> lines[];
private int currentLine;
```

Give an algorithm for adding a wordlet to the current line.

Give an algorithm for moving to the next line.

Reading Words

While parsing the words in the text file is similar to reading the words from the dictionary, it will turn out that using a `StringTokenizer` will make the job easier. A double loop will be employed. A `Scanner` will be used to read the lines and a `StringTokenizer` will be used to break up each line. Consider the following lines of text.

```
Just some fun text! (You shouldn't take it seriously.)

Slowly she turned and said, "Bob, I don't know

if I like you any more. Do you know why?"

He replied "As the raven once said: 'Never more'".
```

Draw boxes around all the words.

What characters in the text indicated the beginning or end of a word (delimiters)?

Are there other characters that might be delimiters?

In our application, we would like to mark words that could be incorrectly spelled within a given body of text. This means that we will not be able to just read words (and discard the delimeters), but will need to read everything into a wordlet.

Review the API for StringTokenizer and show how one can be created that satisfies the preceding observations.

Give an algorithm that will read a file and create wordlets. Add each wordlet to the lines display. At the end of every line, go to the next line in the lines display. Do not worry about checking the spelling.

Algorithm:

Checking the Spelling

Some of the words that the string tokenizer will produce will be things like "!" and "120". The application will assume that if a word has no alpha characters in it, it should not be marked as incorrect.

Write an algorithm that given a string will return true if all the characters are not alpha characters. The isLetter() method in the Character class can be useful here.

Directed Lab Work

Loading the Dictionary

All of the classes needed for the `MisspellApplication` exist. Some of them need to be completed. This application is based on the animated application framework. If you have not already, you should look at the description of it in Appendix A. The classes that you will be completing are `LinesToDisplay` and `MisspellActionThread`. The `Wordlet` class is also specific to this application. Take a look at that code now if you have not done so already.

In the labs so far, no file input or output has been done. Today's application will read from two files. Different Java run time environments use different directories as their default when opening a file. It might be the directory that the class is in or it may be somewhere else. The first goal is to find where the default directory is.

Step 1. Compile and then run `main` from the class `FindDefaultDirectory`.

Step 2. Leave your Java environment temporarily and search for the file name *DefDirHere.txt*.

Step 3. Move the files *sampleDictionary.txt* and *check.txt* to the directory your particular implementation of Java reads from and writes to.

Step 4. Compile the class `MisspellApplication`. Run the `main` method in `MisspellApplication`.

Checkpoint: If all has gone well, you should get a graphical user interface with step controls along the top and application setup controls on the bottom. There should be two text fields where you can enter the name of a file containing the dictionary words and another file that contains the text to be checked. Type check.txt for the text file and then press enter. There should be a message indicating that it is now the text file. If not, check to make sure that you copied the file to the correct place. Type sampleDictionary.txt for the dictionary file and then press enter. Again there should be a message confirming the file is readable.

Step 5. In the method `loadDictionary()` in `MisspellActionThread`, add code that will read the words and put them into the dictionary. The dictionary file contains words that are either separated by spaces or lines. A single loop is needed. Refer back to the algorithm you wrote for the Pre-Lab Exercises and complete the code.

Step 6. Just after reading in all the words, print the dictionary to `System.out`.

Step 7. In the method `executeApplication`, add a call to `loadDictionary()`. Immediately after, set the variable `dictionaryLoaded` to `true`. When the application draws itself, it will now indicate that the dictionary has been loaded. Add in the following line of code to make it pauses before continuing. (For questions about the function of this method, see the discussion in Appendix A.)

```
animationPause();
```

Checkpoint: Press step twice. The display should indicate that the dictionary was loaded. The dictionary should be printed on output. Check it against the file.

Completing LinesToDisplay

Step 8. Complete the constructor for the class `LinesToDisplay`.

Step 9. Refer to the Pre-Lab Exercises and complete the code for the method `addWordlet()`.

Step 10. Refer to the Pre-Lab Exercises and complete the code for the method nextLine().

Step 11. In executeApplication in MisspellActionThread, add the following four lines of code.

```
myLines.addWordlet(new Wordlet("abc", true));
myLines.nextLine();
myLines.addWordlet(new Wordlet("def", false));
myLines.nextLine();
```

Checkpoint: Press step three times. The wordlet abc should be in black on one line and def should be in red on the next line. If not, debug the code and retest.

Step 12. Comment out the four lines of code entered in the previous step.

The next goal is to parse the text file into wordlets and put them in the display. For now all words will be considered to have the correct spelling.

Reading Words

Step 13. Refer to the Pre-Lab Exercises and complete the code in the method checkWords(). As each wordlet is created, use checkWord() to determine if the spelling is correct. (It will just return true.)

Step 14. For the animation, add in the line
   animationPause();

just after the call to nextLine(). (Why not put an animation step after adding every wordlet?)

Checkpoint: Step the application. Each line in the text file should appear exactly with all the text in red. If not, debug the code and retest.

The final goal is to check the spelling of the wordlets.

Checking the Spelling

Step 15. Complete the checkWord() method. You will check the word against the dictionary. Return true if the word is in the dictionary.

Checkpoint: Step the application. Each line in the text file should appear exactly. The words in the dictionary should now appear in black.

Step 16. It would be nice if the punctuation did not show up in red. Refer to the algorithm from the Pre-Lab Exercises and add code to checkWord() to return true if the word is all punctuation.

Final checkpoint: Step the application. Most of the punctuation should now be in black.

There are a number of improvements that can be made to this application. See the post-lab exercises for some of them.

Post-Lab Follow-Ups

1. The program does not correctly check proper words that start with an uppercase letter. Modify the spelling checker so that any word in the dictionary that starts in uppercase must always start in uppercase. Any other words may start either in upper or lowercase. This should not affect the display of the lines of text.

2. The program does not correctly handle words that have an apostrophe. Use a tokenizer that does not split on apostrophes. Instead check the beginning and end of the words for nonalpha characters and split those off into wordlets of their own. This should not affect the display of the lines of text.

3. The program does not handle words that have been hyphenated and broken across lines. Check for this situation and combine the two pieces of the hyphenated word and place it on the next line.

4. Write a program that will do automatic correction of text. Read a file that contains sets of words each on a single line. The first word is the correct word and the rest of the words on that line are common misspellings. Display the corrected text with any changed words in green.

5. Write a program that will highlight key words in a Java program in blue. Make sure that key words inside of comments are not highlighted.

6. Use a dictionary to add memoization to the `better()` method in `RecursiveFibonacci`. In memoization, the method checks to see if it has the answer stored in the dictionary. If it does, it will just return the answer. If not, it will do the computation and then, before returning the answer, remember it in the dictionary.

Lab 12 Hash Table Implementation

Goal

In this lab two different collision resolution schemes will be implemented for a hash table and the resulting performance will be compared with that of linear hashing.

Resources

- Chapter 19: Introducing Hashing
- Chapter 20: Hashing as a Dictionary Implementation
- *DictionaryInterface.html*—API documentation for the DictionaryInterface ADT
- *java.sun.com/j2se/1.5.0/docs/api*—API documentation for the java.util.Random class
- *Lab12Graphs.pdf*—Printable versions of the graphs for this lab

Java Files

- *DictionaryInterface.java*
- *HashedDictionaryOpenAddressingLinear.java*
- *CheckSearchHashTable.java*
- *HashPerformance.java*

Introduction

One of the fastest dictionary implementations is the hash table. As long as the table does not become too full, the time for adding and finding an element will be O(1). This performance does not come without some cost. The obvious penalty is that there will be space in the table that is wasted. Another penalty is that the items in the hash table are not in any particular order. Other dictionary implementations will keep items in key order, but it is an inherent property of the hash table that items are not ordered. In fact, as more items are added to the hash table, the size of the table may be increased to maintain the performance. In this case, the items will be rehashed and will no longer be in the same locations or order.

General Collision Resolution

To place an item in a hash table of size m, a hash function H(k, m) is applied to the key k. An integer value between 0 and m–1 will be returned and will be the location of the object. If there is already an object in that location, a collision has occurred and must be resolved. In a hash table with open addressing, collisions are resolved by trying other locations until an empty slot is found. One way of viewing this process is that there is a series of hash functions $H_0()$, $H_1()$, $H_2()$, $H_3()$, ... $H_i()$, ..., which are applied one at a time until a free slot is found.

Linear Hashing

For linear hashing, slots in the hash table are examined one after another. From the view of the general scheme, the hash functions are

$$H_0(k, m) = H(k, m)$$
$$H_1(k, m) = (H(k, m) + 1) \bmod m$$
$$H_2(k, m) = (H(k, m) + 2) \bmod m$$
$$\dots$$
$$H_i(k, m) = (H(k, m) + i) \bmod m$$

The mod operation is required to keep the values in the range from 0 to m−1. While you could use these formulas to compute each of the hash locations, usually the previous value is used to compute the next one.

$$H_i(k, m) = (H_{i-1}(k, m) + 1) \bmod m$$

Linear hashing has the advantage of a simple computational formula that guarantees all the slots will be checked. The performance of linear hashing is affected by the creation of clusters of slots that are filled. Suppose that there are relatively few large clusters. If there is a collision with a slot inside a cluster, getting outside of the cluster will require a large number of probes. For the best performance, the free slots should be distributed evenly and large clusters avoided.

Pre-Lab Visualization

Double Hashing

Double hashing is scheme for resolving collisions that uses two hash functions $H(k, m)$ and $h(k,m)$. It is similar to linear hashing except that instead of changing the index by 1, the value of the second hash function is used.

From the view of the general scheme, the hash functions are
$$H_0(k, m) = H(k, m)$$
$$H_1(k, m) = (H(k, m) + h(k,m)) \bmod m$$
$$H_2(k, m) = (H(k, m) + 2\, h(k,m)) \bmod m$$
...
$$H_i(k, m) = (H(k, m) + i\, h(k,m)) \bmod m$$

As with linear hashing, the hash function can be defined in terms of the previous values.
$$H_i(k, m) = (H_{i-1}(k, m) + h(k,m)) \bmod m$$

You must be careful when defining the second hash function.

Suppose that $H(k, m)$ is 12, $h(k,m) = 0$, and $m = 15$. What are the locations that will be probed?

$H_0(k, m)$	$H_1(k, m)$	$H_2(k, m)$	$H_3(k, m)$	$H_4(k, m)$	$H_5(k, m)$

Suppose that $H(k, m)$ is 12, $h(k,m) = 4$, and $m = 15$. What are the locations that will be probed?

$H_0(k, m)$	$H_1(k, m)$	$H_2(k, m)$	$H_3(k, m)$	$H_4(k, m)$	$H_5(k, m)$

If m=15, which values of $h(k,m)$ will visit all of the locations in the table?

h(k,m)	0	1	2	3	4	5	6	7	8	9	10	11	12	13	14	15
Visits all locations?																

Since you really want to probe the entire table, the value returned by the second hash function has some limitations. The first condition is that it should not be 0. The second condition is that it should be relatively prime with respect to m. A common way to guarantee the second condition is to choose a table size that is a prime.

Suppose that you have access to an integer value c that is based on the key
c=HashCode(k).

The first hash function will be computed as
H(k,m) = c mod m.

Under the assumption that m is a prime, give a formula for computing a second hash function using c. It should return values in the range of 1 to m–1.

Double hashing can still be affected by clustering (though to a lesser extent than linear hashing). Every key that has the same value for the second key will probe the table in the same pattern and can still be affected by clusters.

Show how to modify the following code so that it computes the second hash value and then uses it in the search.

```
private int locate(int index, T key)
{
    boolean found = false;

    while ( !found && (hashTable[index] != null) )
    {
        if ( hashTable[index].isIn() &&
                 key.equals(hashTable[index].getKey()) )
            found = true; // key found
        else // follow probe sequence
            index = (index + 1) % hashTable.length; //linear probing
    } // end while

    // Assertion: either key is found or a
    // null location is reached
    int result = -1;

    if (found)
        result = index;

    return result;
} // end locate
```

Perfect Hashing

In perfect hashing, associated with each key is a unique random sequence of probe locations. Since each key has a unique "view" of the table, the locations of the free slots will be randomly spread out and clustering will be avoided. Even though an approximation to perfect hashing will be implemented in the lab, it is mainly of theoretical interest because perfect hashing is much easier to analyze than linear or double hashing.

Let $s_0(k)$, $s_1(k)$, $s_2(k)$, ... be a random sequence of values in the range 0 to m–1.

$$H_0(k, m) = s_0(k)$$
$$H_1(k, m) = s_1(k)$$
$$H_2(k, m) = s_2(k)$$
...
$$H_i(k, m) = s_i(k)$$

A truly random sequence is not possible, but you can approximate it using pseudo random numbers. Most algorithmic random number generators use the following simple formula to compute a sequence of numbers:

$$V_{n+1} = (aV_n+c) \bmod m$$

Given that a = 3, c = 2, and m = 10, what is the sequence of numbers computed?

V_0	V_1	V_2	V_3	V_4	V_5	V_6	V_7
3							

Is the preceding sequence random? No. It follows a prescribed sequence. If you know one value in the sequence, you know the next value. Further, notice that the preceding sequence misses some of the values between 0 and 9. This means it would not be suitable for a random number generator. In fact, most values for a, c, and m do not result in good pseudorandom number generators, so it is best not to choose your own values. Instead, either use a professionally designed random number generator or use one of the published sets of values that have passed a thorough battery of statistical tests.

Even though the sequence is not random, for good choices of values it can appear random which is sufficient for our algorithm. In addition, the fact that the values are actually not random is crucial for the implementation of the perfect hashing algorithm. Each time a value is searched for, you must follow exactly the same sequence. The first value in the sequence is called the seed. If you initialize the pseudorandom number generator with a given seed, it will always produce the same sequence of numbers. This will be the basis for the probe sequence used in perfect hashing.

Show how you can create a new random number generator of the type Random from the package java.util. Use c = HashCode(k) as the seed for the random number generator.

Show how to modify the following code so that instead of receiving a starting index it gets a random number generator. To find the index use the method nextInt(int k) method with k as the table size. This will guarantee a random value in the range of 0 to k–1.

```
private int locate(int index, T key)
{
    boolean found = false;

    while ( !found && (hashTable[index] != null) )
    {
        if ( hashTable[index].isIn() &&
                key.equals(hashTable[index].getKey()) )
            found = true; // key found
        else // follow probe sequence
            index = (index + 1) % hashTable.length; //linear probing
    } // end while

    // Assertion: either key is found or a
    // null location is reached
    int result = -1;

    if (found)
        result = index;

    return result;
} // end locate
```

Creating Random Search Keys

The average time to locate a value in a hash table is usually given based on whether the value is in the table or not. To insert a new value in a table, you must probe for a free slot. Thus the time to insert a new value is basically the same as the time to search for a value that is not in the table. To search for a value that is in the table, you must follow the same pattern of probes that was used when the value was inserted. The average will include values that were inserted early and thus require few probes to locate. This average will be less than the average number of probes required to determine that a value is not in the table.

To test both kinds of searches, an array of unique random words will be created. The first half of the array will be inserted into a hash table. The average of finding a value in the first half of the array will give the average for successful searches and the average over the second half will give the average for unsuccessful (failure) searches.

To make the test more interesting, random three-syllable pseudowords will be created. It is possible that a word will be generated twice. To avoid placing such words in the array, you will have to test to see if the word has been generated before. Using a hash table is a perfect way to do this. As a word is generated, check the hash table to see if it has been generated before. If not, add it to the array and the hash table.

Write an algorithm that creates the array of unique random words. You may assume that three arrays of syllables `firstSyl`, `secondSyl`, and `thirdSyl` have already been created. Further, assume that a random number generator of type `Random` from the package `java.util` has been created. It may be helpful to use the method `nextInt(int k)` which will return a random integer from 0 to k–1.

The Average Number of Words Generated to Get a Unique Word

One thing to consider is the number of words that will be generated before a unique value is found. As more unique words are generated, it becomes more and more likely that you will randomly generate a previously created word and have to discard it. This may become too much of a burden. Let's find out how much of a burden it will be.

To do so, the probability that more than one word will be generated will have to be computed. Probabilities are real values between 0 and 1. It tells you the likelihood that an event occurs. An event with a probability of 0.5 has a 50% chance of occurring. An event with a probability of 1 is certain.

Suppose that there are a total of T = 1000 unique words that can be created. (In general, T will be the sizes of the three syllable arrays multiplied together.) Suppose further that 600 words have already been generated.

What is the probability that a randomly generated word will be one that has been generated before?

What is the probability that a randomly generated word will not be one that has been generated before?

To determine the average number of words that will need to be generated in order to get a unique word, one must consider all the possible events (number of words generated to get the unique word) along with their probabilities. Multiplying the number of words needed for each event by the corresponding probability and then adding all the products together gives the average. Let's create a table with that information (under the assumption that 600 of 1000 unique words have been found already).

Event	Probability	Value	Product
1 word generated			
2 words generated			
3 words generated			
4 words generated			
5 words generated			
6 words generated			
7 words generated			
8 words generated			
9 words generated			
...			

The probability that only one word is generated will be just the probability that the first word generated is not one that has been generated before. Write that probability in the table.

The probability that two words are generated will be the product of the probability that the first word had been generated before times the probability that the second word was not generated before. Write that probability in the table.

The probability that three words are generated will be the product of the probability that the first word had been generated before times the probability that the second word had been generated before times the probability that the third word was not generated before. Write that probability in the table.

There is a pattern here. Using that pattern complete the probabilities column in the table.

Lab 12   Hash Table Implementation

The values will just be the number of words generated. Fill in that value column in the table.

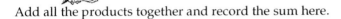

For each row in the table multiply the probability by the value and record the result in the product column.

Add all the products together and record the sum here.

To get the exact answer, you must add up an infinite number of terms. The product is composed of two parts. One part is getting smaller exponentially and the other is getting larger linearly. Eventually the exponential part will dominate and the sum will converge. For the given situation, nine terms will give an answer that is reasonably close to the exact value of 2.5.

As long as no more than 60% of the possible words have been generated, the number of extra words that get generated will be less than 1.5 and will not be too much of a burden on our algorithm.

The syllable arrays given in the lab each have a size of 15. How many possible words are there?

What is 60% of this total?

To test hash tables with more data values than this, the size of the syllable arrays will need to be increased.

Counting the Number of Probes

Consider again the code that locates an item or a free slot in the hash table using linear probing.

```
private int locate(int index, T key)
{
    boolean found = false;

    while( !found && (hashTable[index] != null) )
    {
        if ( hashTable[index].isIn() &&
                key.equals(hashTable[index].getKey()) )
            found = true; // key found
        else // follow probe sequence
                index = (index + 1) % hashTable.length //linear probing
    } // end while

    // Assertion: either key is found or a
    // null location is reached
    int result = -1;

    if (found)
        result = index;

    return result;
} // end locate
```

Suppose that index is 2 and key is 57. Trace the code and circle the index of any location that is accessed.

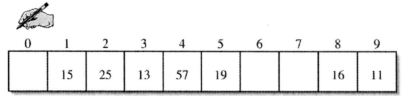

How many locations were circled? (How many probes were made?)

How many times did the body of the loop execute?

Now suppose index is 2 and key is 99. Trace the code again and circle the index of any location that is accessed.

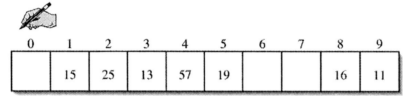

How many locations were circled? (How many probes were made?)

How many times did the body of the loop execute?

It should be the case that only one of the traces had the same number of loop executions as probes.

Show how to modify the `locate()` method given previously so that it will add the number of probes made to a static variable named `totalProbes`.

Directed Lab Work

A hash table class with linear collision resolution has already been implemented in the `HashedDictionaryOpenAddressingLinear` class.

You will implement three new classes `HashedDictionaryOpenAddressingLinearInstrumented`, `HashedDictionaryOpenAddressingDoubleInstrumented`, and `HashedDictionaryOpenAddressingPerfectInstrumented`

based on that class. They will allow you to gather statistics about the number of probes made to insert values. The `HashPerformance` class will generate random arrays of keys, insert the keys in the various kinds of hash tables, and then display the averages.

Implementing Double Hashing

Step 1. If you have not done so, look at the implementation of a hash table with linear probing in *HashedDictionaryOpenAddressingLinear.java*.

Also take a look at the code in *CheckSearchHashTable.java*. Compile both the classes `CheckSearchHashTable` and `HashedDictionaryOpenAddressingLinear`. Run the `main()` method in `CheckSearchHashTable`.

Checkpoint: The program will ask you for the number of trials, the number of data values, and a seed. Enter 1, 1000, and 123, respectively. An array of 1000 random values between 0 and 1000 should be generated. The first 500 of those values will be inserted into a hash table. The code will check that searches work correctly. The first 250 values in the array will then be removed from the hash table. Again searches will be checked. Finally, the last 500 values in the array will be added into the hash table. Again searches will be checked.

Verify that the code passed each of the three tests.

The first goal is to create the class for double hashing and verify that it works.

Step 2. Copy *HashedDictionaryOpenAddressingLinear.java* into a new file *HashedDictionaryOpenAddressingDoubleInstrumented.java*.

Step 3. Create a new private method `getSecondHashIndex(Object key)`, which computes a second hash function. Refer to the formula created in the Pre-Lab exercises.

Step 4. Refer to the Pre-Lab exercises and modify the `locate()` and `probe()` methods to use double hashing instead of linear hashing.

Step 5. Change the code in `CheckSearchHashTable` so that it creates a new object of type `HashedDictionaryOpenAddressingDoubleInstrumented`.

Run the main method in `CheckSearchHashTable`.

Checkpoint: Use 1, 1000, and 123 for the input values.

Verify that the code passed each of the three tests. If not, debug the code and retest.

The next goal is to create the class for perfect hashing and verify that it works.

Implementing Perfect Hashing

Step 6. Copy `HashedDictionaryOpenAddressingLinear.java` into a new file `HashedDictionaryOpenAddressingPerfectInstrumented.java`.

Step 7. Create a new private method `getHashGenerator(Object key)` which will create the random number generator used to generate the sequence of probes. Refer to your answer from the Pre-Lab exercise.

Step 8. Again, refer to the Pre-Lab exercises and modify the `locate()` and `probe()` methods to use perfect hashing instead of linear hashing. (Remember to change the first argument to be a random number generator instead of an integer.)

Step 9. Find all places where the `locate()` and `probe()` methods are called and change it so that `getHashGenerator` is called invoked instead of `getHashIndex`. Once you are finished, there should no longer be any calls to `getHashIndex`. Remove the `getHashIndex` method.

Step 10. Change the code in `CheckSearchHashTable` so that it creates a new object of type `HashedDictionaryOpenAddressingPerfectInstrumented`.

Run the main method in `CheckSearchHashTable`.

Checkpoint: Use 1, 1000, and 123 for the input values.

Verify that the code still passes each of the three tests. If not, debug the code and retest.

Adding Statistics

Step 11.   Copy *HashedDictionaryOpenAddressingLinear.java* into a new file *HashedDictionaryOpenAddressingLinearInstrumented.java*.

Step 12.   Refer to the Pre-Lab exercises and add in code to the `locate()` and `probe()` methods that will count the number of probes.

Step 13.   Change the code in `CheckSearchHashTable` so that it creates a new object of type `HashedDictionaryOpenAddressingLinearInstrumented`.

Run the `main` method in `CheckSearchHashTable`.

Checkpoint: Use 1, 1000, and 123 for the input values.

Verify that the code still passes each of the three tests. If not, debug the code and retest.

Step 14.   Make similar changes in `HashedDictionaryOpenAddressingDoubleInstrumented` and `HashedDictionaryOpenAddressingPerfectInstrumented`.

Step 15.   Change the code in `CheckSearchHashTable` so that it creates a new object of type `HashedDictionaryOpenAddressingDoubleInstrumented`. Run the `main()` method in `CheckSearchHashTable`.

Checkpoint: Use 1, 1000, and 123 for the input values.

Verify that the code still passes each of the three tests. If not, debug the code and retest.

Step 16.   Change the code in `CheckSearchHashTable` so that it creates a new object of type `HashedDictionaryOpenAddressingPerfectInstrumented`. Run the `main()` method in `CheckSearchHashTable`.

Checkpoint: Use 1, 1000, and 123 for the input values.

Verify that the code still passes each of the three tests. If not, debug the code and retest.

Generating Random Keys

Step 17.   Finish the method `generateRandomData()` in the class `HashPerformance`. Refer to the algorithm in the Pre-Lab exercises.

Step 18.   Compile the code in `HashPerformance` and run the `main()` method.

Checkpoint: The code will ask for the number of items to insert, the number of trials, and the maximum load factor for the hash table. Use 1, 10, and 0.9 for the input values.

If all has gone well, the total number of probes will be 10 and the average will be 1.

Checkpoint: The code will ask for the number of items to insert, the number of trials, and the maximum load factor for the hash table. Use 10, 10, and 0.9 for the input values.

If all has gone well, the total number of probes will be approximately 105 and the average will be 1.05. Check that the strings in each array are all different.

Checkpoint: The code will ask for the number of items to insert, the number of trials, and the maximum load factor for the hash table. Use 80, 10, and 0.9 for the input values.

If all has gone well, the total number of probes for linear hashing will be approximately 2200. The total number of probes for double and perfect hashing should be about 1550. In general, perfect hashing is expected to take slightly fewer probes than double hashing.

Insert Performance

Step 19. Run HashPerformance for different numbers of items to be inserted into the hash table and record the results in the following two tables. In each case, enter 10 for the number of trials and 0.5 for the maximum load for the hash table.

Average Number of Probes for the Three Kinds of Hash Tables

NUMBER OF ITEMS INSERTED	AVERAGE PROBES FOR LINEAR HASHING	AVERAGE PROBES FOR DOUBLE HASHING	AVERAGE PROBES FOR PERFECT HASHING
10			
20			
30			
40			
50			
60			
70			
80			
90			
100			
110			

You should notice a sudden jump in the number of probes needed. The hash table resizing itself and then rehashing all the items causes this. The average cost for the insertions after a resize will show a decrease as the cost of the resizing is spread out over the insertions that follow. At approximately what values did a resizing occur?

Average Number of Probes for the Three Kinds of Hash Tables

NUMBER OF ITEMS INSERTED	AVERAGE PROBES FOR LINEAR HASHING	AVERAGE PROBES FOR DOUBLE HASHING	AVERAGE PROBES FOR PERFECT HASHING
100			
200			
300			
400			
500			
600			
700			
800			
900			
1000			

Step 20. Plot the average number of probes for each of the three kinds of hash tables on the following two graphs.

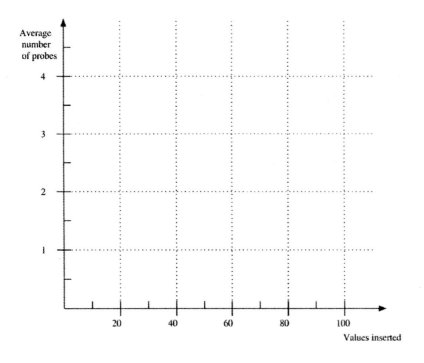

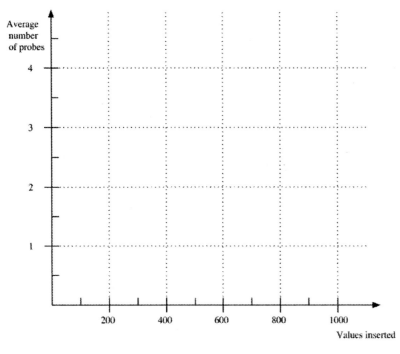

Insertion Performance versus Initial Table Size

The cost of resizing the table is a hidden cost that gets spread out over all of the insertions. If you can accurately predict the number of data values to be inserted, this hidden cost can be avoided by setting the initial size of the table to be larger.

Step 21. In the class HashPerformance, add code that will query the user for the initial size of the hash table. It should be a positive integer value.

Step 22. Modify the invocation of the constructor for each of the three kinds of hash tables to take as an argument the value that was read in.

Step 23. Run HashPerformance for different initial sizes of the hash table and record the results. In each case, enter 1000 for the number of items to insert, 10 for the number of trials, and 0.5 for the maximum load.

Average Number of Probes with Respect to the Initial Table Size

INITIAL TABLE SIZE	AVERAGE PROBES FOR LINEAR HASHING	AVERAGE PROBES FOR DOUBLE HASHING	AVERAGE PROBES FOR PERFECT HASHING
50			
100			
250			
500			
1000			
2000			

In each of the cases, the final size of the hash table will be about 2000.

Step 24. Plot the data on the following graph.

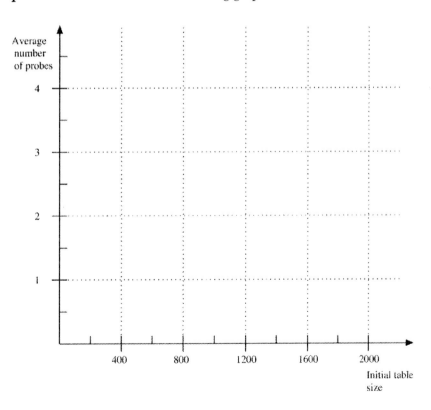

Search Performance versus Load Factor

The cost of searching for an item in a hash table is not affected by resizing. Code will be added to distinguish between the number of probes required to search for items in the table (successful search) and items that are not in the table (failure or unsuccessful search).

Step 25. In the class HashPerformance, add a method insertHalfData() that is based on insertAllData(). It will insert just the first half of the array into the hash table.

Step 26. In the class HashPerformance, add the methods searchFirstHalf() and searchSecondHalf() that search for each of the keys in the first and second half of the array, respectively. Use the method contains() to determine if the value is in the hash table.

Step 27. Change the call to generateRandomData() so that it uses 2*insertCount instead of insertCount.

Step 28. Change the code in the main() of HashPerformance so that it calls insertHalfData() instead of insertAllData().

Step 29. After the code that records the number of probes for the insertions, add code that calls resetTotalProbes, performs searchFirstHalf, and then finally records the number of probes needed for the *successful searches*. Do this for each of the three kinds of hash tables.

Step 30. After that code, add code that calls resetTotalProbes, performs searchSecondHalf, and finally records the number of probes needed for the *unsuccessful searches*. Do this for each of the three kinds of hash tables.

Step 31. Compile and run HashPerformance.

Checkpoint: Enter 100 for the number of values to insert, 1000 for the number of trials, 0.75 for the maximum load factor, and 75 for the initial table size.

The values should be close (typically a difference between –0.1 to 0.1) to the ones listed in the following table. If the values are close but not within the desired range, run the code again with the same values and recheck the results. If the values are still not close, carefully examine the code for errors.

	Average Number of Probes to Insert the Data	Average Number of Probes for Successful Searches	Average Number of Probes for Unsuccessful Searches
Linear Hashing	3.1	1.7	3.6
Double Hashing	2.6	1.5	2.6
Perfect Hashing	2.6	1.5	2.6

Step 32. Compile and run HashPerformance for different load factors. The load factor is the number of data items in the table divided by the table size. The initial table size and maximum load factor will be chosen so that the table does not resize and the desired load factor is achieved once all the values have been inserted into the hash table. In each case, enter 10 for the number of trials, 0.99 for the maximum load for the hash table, and 1000 for the initial table size.

Average Number of Probes for Successful Searches

LOAD FACTOR (N = NUMBER OF DATA VALUES TO INSERT)	AVERAGE PROBES FOR LINEAR HASHING	AVERAGE PROBES FOR DOUBLE HASHING	AVERAGE PROBES FOR PERFECT HASHING
0.30 (n=300)			
0.40 (n=400)			
0.50 (n=500)			
0.60 (n=600)			
0.70 (n=700)			
0.75 (n=750)			
0.80 (n=800)			
0.85 (n=850)			
0.90 (n=900)			
0.95 (n=950)			

Average Number of Probes for Failed Searches

LOAD FACTOR	AVERAGE PROBES FOR LINEAR HASHING	AVERAGE PROBES FOR DOUBLE HASHING	AVERAGE PROBES FOR PERFECT HASHING
0.30 (n=300)			
0.40 (n=400)			
0.50 (n=500)			
0.60 (n=600)			
0.70 (n=700)			
0.75 (n=750)			
0.80 (n=800)			
0.85 (n=850)			
0.90 (n=900)			
0.95 (n=950)			

Step 33. Plot the data on the following graphs.

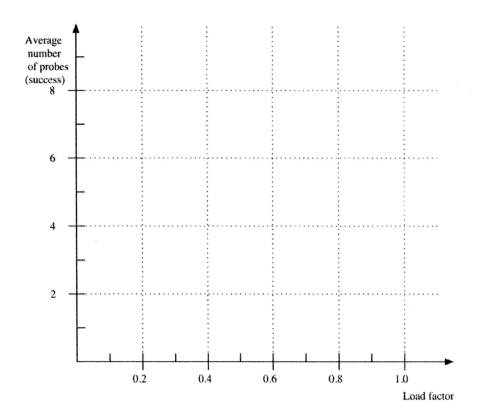

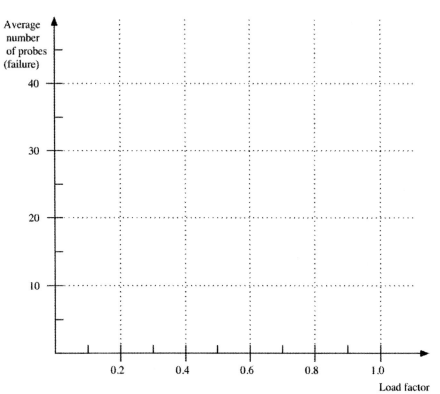

Lab 12   Hash Table Implementation

Post-Lab Follow-Ups

1. Add two methods `startSearch()` and `endSearch()` to the instrumented hash table classes. The method `startSearch()` will be called at the beginning of `locate()` and `probe()`. The method `endSearch()` will be called at the end of `locate()` and `probe()`. Use these methods to compute the maximum and minimum numbers of probes needed by `locate()` and `probe()`.

2. Use the methods added in the pervious exercise to compute the standard deviation of the number of probes needed.

3. Change the `rehash()` method so that it increases the size of the hash table by a constant value (set it to the initial size of the hash table.) Recalculate the insertion performance of the three kinds of hash tables and plot.

4. Change the `rehash()` method so that it increases the size of the hash table by a constant factor (set it to 20%). Recalculate the insertion performance of the three kinds of hash tables and plot.

5. Create a new class that implements quadratic hashing. Add code to count the number of probes. Compute the performance and plot.

6. Create code that will test the performance of a hash table when there are insertions and deletions. Start by adding N values to the table. Then do a sequence of K operations. For each operation, randomly choose to add or remove a value with a probability of 0.5. Print the number of probes needed for the K operations. Once the K operations are finished, compute the performance of the resulting table for successful and unsuccessful searches. Plot the results for K = 100, 1000, and 10000 with values of N that are 200, 400, 600, 800, 1000.

7. Add code to the hash table classes that will create a smaller table and rehash. Add code that keeps track of the slots that are empty but marked as removed. Compute a load factor that is based on the number of filled slots plus the number of slots marked as removed. If this value ever gets larger than the maximum load factor, rehash the table.

   Insert N items into the table initially. Compute the performance with and without this rehashing when adding and removing K blocks of M randomly chosen items.

8. Each random word that was created can be represented as a triplet of three numbers. Create a method that given a triplet will create the next one in a lexicographic order. Given a random triplet as a starting point, use this method to generate words without any repetition. To make the words look more random, you can skip over K triplets and as long as K is relatively prime with respect to the total number of possible triplets, every triplet will be visited before there is a repetition. (This is similar to the search pattern that double hashing does.)

9. If perfect hashing into a table with load factor $\alpha = N / M$ has a probability of $1 - \alpha$ of finding an empty slot, compute the average number of probes needed to find an empty slot. The computation is similar to the one done in the Pre-Lab to determine the average number of random words you must generate to get a unique word when duplicates are to be discarded. This computation can be done exactly.

Lab 13 Stack Client

Goal

In this lab you will use a stack to create an iterative version of quick sort. Then an animated program that will be completed that searches for a target square in a maze.

Resources

- Chapter 12: Faster Sorting Methods
- Chapter 21: Stacks
- *java.sun.com/j2se/1.5.0/docs/api*—API documentation for the Java Stack class
- *Maze.html*—API documentation for the class Maze, which contains all the maze data
- *Maze.jar*—The working application
- *Lab13Graphs.pdf*—Printable versions of the graphs for this lab

Java Files

Files in Directory Sorts:
- *IterativeFibonacci.java*
- *TestFibonacci.java*
- *SortArray.java*
- *CheckSort.java*
- *TimeSort.java*

Files in Directory Maze:
- *MazeApplication.java*
- *MazeActionThread.java*
- *Maze.java*

There are other files used to animate the application. For a full description, see Appendix A.

Input Files

- *maze1.java*
- *maze2.java*
- *maze3.java*
- *maze4.java*
- *maze5.java*
- *maze6.java*

Introduction

In computer science, one of the important basic structures is the stack. In its simplest form it has three operations: push, pop, and empty. Push places a value on the top of the stack. Pop removes the top value from the stack. Empty is a test to determine if the stack has any values in it. Some specifications have a fourth operation called peek (or top). Peek will return the top value on the stack but leaves the number of items unchanged. Strictly speaking, peek is unnecessary because a pop followed by a push will mimic its operation.

In theoretical computer science, one of the problems of interest is recognizing words in a language. In this context, a language is a set of words that follow some pattern. For example, one language is all the words from the alphabet {0, 1} that have equal numbers of zeros and ones. The word 001011 is in the language, but the word 00111 is not.

There are a number of primitive models of computation that have different abilities. One kind of model is a machine called a pushdown automata (PDA). It has a finite control (program) and a single stack that it can use for memory.

While fairly powerful, a PDA does have some surprising limits. For example, while a PDA can recognize words of the form 0^n1^n, it cannot recognize $0^n\ 1^n\ 0^n$. Modern computer languages are often recursively defined by a grammar, which can be recognized by a PDA.

There is a strong relation between stacks and recursion. The desire to do recursive computations easily has impacted computer hardware. The architecture of modern computers has a built-in stack. A method call will place the return address on the stack. Variables for the method will be stored on the stack as well.

Converting Recursion to Iteration

Recall the code that computes the Fibonacci sequence (from Lab 6). A couple of temporary variables that are often generated by the compiler are made explicit in the following version.

```
int F(int n)
{
    int temp1;
    int temp2;
    int result;

    if( n <= 0)
        result = 0;
    else if (n == 1)
        result = 1;
    else
    {
        temp1 = F(n-1);
        temp2 = F(n-2);
        result = temp1 + temp2;
    }
    return result;
}
```

Look at the pattern of recursive calls for the computation of F(3).

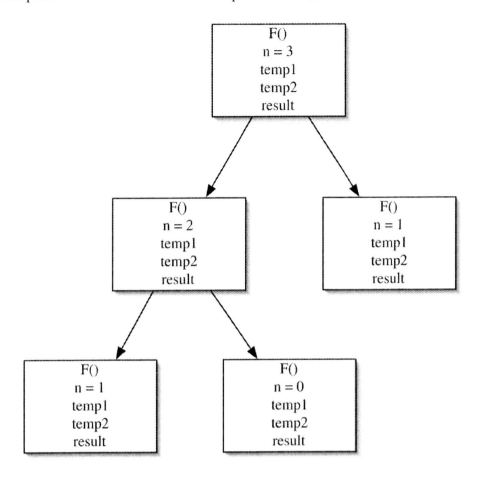

Each recursive call of F() will have its own copies of the variables n, temp1, temp2, and result. Let's trace the operation of the code and keep frames for each of the sets of variables off to the side.

Call F(3)

F(3) - frame1

frame 1
n = 3
temp1
temp2
result

The if statement is evaluated and the next recursive call is made. While the new version of F() is executing, the variables for F(3) must be kept safe, but they do not need to be accessed.

Call F(2)

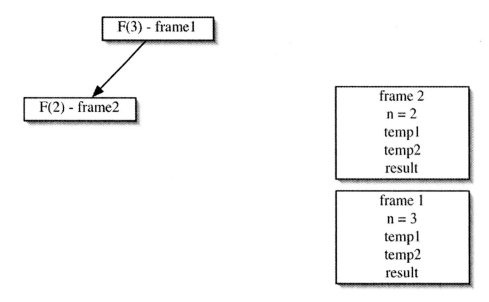

Again, the if statement is evaluated and the next recursive call is made. While the new version of F() is executing, the variables for F(3) and F(2) must be kept safe, but they do not need to be accessed.

Call F(1)

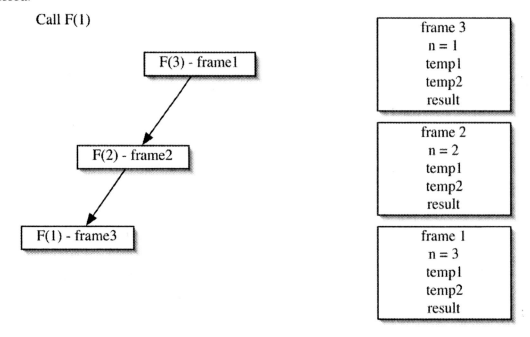

This time the base case is reached. The computation sets the value of result in frame 3 and then F(1) returns. The returned value is stored in temp1 of frame 2.

F(1) returns

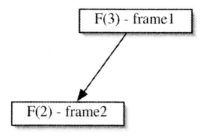

frame 3
n = 1
temp1
temp2
result = 1

frame 2
n = 2
temp1=1
temp2
result

frame 1
n = 3
temp1
temp2
result

The variables in frame 3 are no longer needed. It will be disposed of.

Dispose of frame 3

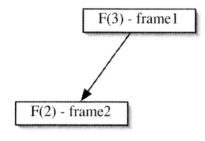

frame 2
n = 2
temp1=1
temp2
result

frame 1
n = 3
temp1
temp2
result

The computation for F(2) continues. It makes a recursive call to F(0).

Call F(0)

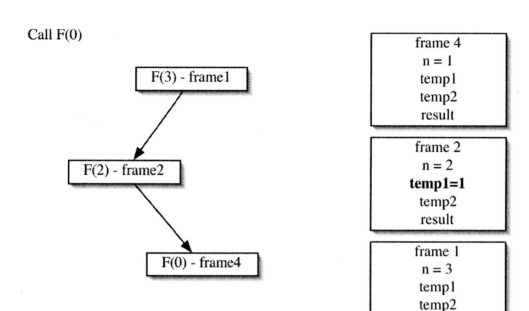

Jumping ahead a bit, F(0) will finish and frame 4 can be released.

Dispose of frame 4

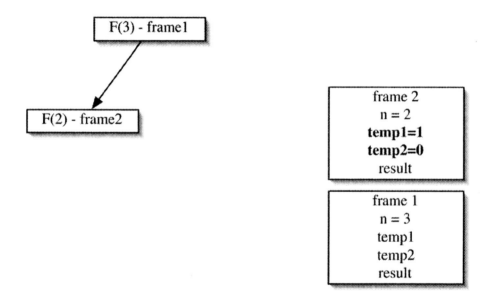

Now that F(2) has both its values, it will compute result and then return. Frame 2 will be disposed now.

It is easy to see that the frames can be stored on a stack. Each time a call is made, the new frame is pushed on the stack. Each time a return is made, a frame is popped off the top of the stack. At any time, only the top frame on the stack will be accessed.

This all happens automatically for the recursive program. But there is another choice. The computation can be done iteratively using an explicit stack.

On the stack will be stored the same frames, but there is one extra item that is needed. When the call to F(0) returned, how did the computation know where to put the value? There was a return address that was also stored on the stack that gives the correct place to resume the computation. That will need to be coded in a variable. Each recursive call separates the code into sections. Let's call the sections START, USE1, and USE2. At each iterative step, the top item on the stack is removed and the appropriate computation is done. When a recursive call is encountered, two frames are placed on the stack. The first is the frame for the current computation with the section that will be performed next. The second is the frame for the recursive call. When a frame finishes, it puts its result into a shared variable *result* that is used to hold the return value.

The basic algorithm is as follows:
1. Put the first frame on the stack.
2. While the stack is not empty
   a. Take the top frame from the stack.
   b. Do the computation indicated by the section.
   c. If a recursive call is needed.
      i. Put the current frame on the stack with the status set to indicate the state of the computation.
      ii. Put a start frame on the stack for the recursive call
   d. If the computation is finished, place the returned value in *result*.
3. Return *result*.

The iteration continues until there are no more frames on the stack. The first iterations for Fibonacci are

		frame 3 n = 1 temp1 temp2 result s = START		frame 4 n = 0 temp1 temp2 result s = START
	frame 2 n = 2 temp1 temp2 result s = START	frame 2 n = 3 temp1 temp2 result s = USE1	frame 2 n = 3 temp1 temp2 result s = USE1	frame 2 n = 3 **temp1 = 1** temp2 result s = USE2
frame 1 n = 3 temp1 temp2 result s = START	frame 1 n = 3 temp1 temp2 result s = USE1	frame 1 n = 3 temp1 temp2 result s = USE1	frame 1 n = 3 temp1 temp2 result s = USE1	frame 1 n = 3 temp1 temp2 result s = USE1
Before Iteration 1	Before Iteration 2	Before Iteration 3	Before Iteration 4	Before Iteration 5

The code is a bit intimidating, but it works. It is in *IterativeFibonacci.java* in the lab folder, so you can look at it and verify that it is correct. One of the advantages of using the recursion provided by Java is an economy of expression. One might ask: "Why do it iteratively then?" One answer is that doing recursive method calls may be more expensive than iteration with the stack. Unfortunately, this iterative version of Fibonacci mimics the doubly recursive method, so it will have the same bad exponential performance. It may be slightly faster than the recursive version, but it is still horrible.

Pre-Lab Visualization

Quick Sort

The technique described previously can be applied to quick sort.

Look at the code for version3QuickSort() in SortArray.

Candidates to be stored on the stack:

What are the parameters of the method?

What are the local variables of the method?

Does it matter which order the recursive sorts are performed in?

Quick sort is a little easier to convert than Fibonacci from above. The reason is that Fibonacci requires knowledge of which recursive call was made so it can correctly perform the combine logic. Quick sort basically has no combine logic. Once it has finished the split logic, it can schedule both recursive calls.

Does the array need to be in the frame or can there be a single variable for the array shared by all the calls?

Is the local variable `pivotIndex` required after the recursive calls are scheduled? (If not, it does not need to be in the frame.)

At this point, the only variables that seem to be required in the frame are `first` and `last`.

Give an algorithm for an iterative version of quick sort. (Remember, no switch statement is needed. Just take in a chunk to process, process it, and (if needed) put two new chunks out.)

Trace its operation on the array:

6	2	10	7	4	3	1	9	5	8

Maze Recursion

Suppose there is a maze. Robo-rat is placed in the maze. A battery is placed in a different location in the maze. Robo-rat needs to search to find the battery. In the following picture, the starting location of Robo-rat is the star and the battery is the double circle.

Where can Robo-rat go from here? He has four choices for direction: north, south, east, and west. Suppose Robo-rat chooses to go west.

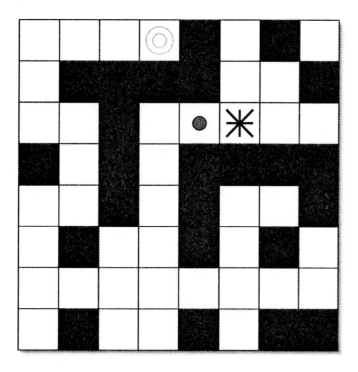

Where does Robo-rat go now? Does anything prevent him from going back east? Clearly, he needs to mark the positions that he visits so he doesn't visit them again. But there were four directions he could have chosen at the first step; how can he get back to them?

Recursion is useful here. To search the maze, Robo-rat can recursively search each of the four directions. If he is unsuccessful in one direction, eventually that recursive call will return. The next recursive call is made and off Robo-rat goes again searching the next direction. The backtracking that is needed is accomplished naturally by the recursion.

Give a recursive design for searching in a maze. Assume that there are primitive operations that allow you to

- mark the square Robo-rat is in,
- check to see if a neighbor square is marked,
- check to see if a neighbor square has a wall,
- move Robo-rat to a neighbor square,
- and backtrack Robo-rat to a square he has previously visited.

At the end, Robo-rat should be in the same square as the battery (if a path to the battery exists).

 Identify the problem:

 Identify the smaller problems:

 Identify how the answers are composed:

 Identify the base cases:

 Compose the recursive definition:

Show the order that the squares are visited in the preceding maze.

Iterative Maze Search

The iterative maze search will be similar in many respects to the iterative quick sort.

Does the order that directions are searched matter?

Is the composition of the subproblems nontrivial?

As with quick sort, the iterative version does not need to keep a status. It just needs to keep the next location to check on the stack.

Give an iterative algorithm for maze search that uses a stack. The same primitives are available as before.

Trace the algorithm on the following maze. Mark the order that squares are visited.

For the lab, one slight modification will be made. Anytime a square is placed on the stack as a potential direction, it will be marked as scheduled. Robo-rat will not visit a scheduled square until he finally takes it off of the stack.

With this modification, trace the algorithm on the following maze. Again, mark the order that squares are visited.

Directed Lab Work

Creating Iterative Quick Sort

The basic and advanced sorts have been implemented in the SortArray *class. The class* CheckSort *will generate some arrays, call a sorting routine, and check that it correctly sorts the values. The class* TimeSort *will be used to time the sorts.*

Step 1.   Create a new class named QSFrame. (Don't create it inside of SortArray. This will avoid some problems with the static sorting methods.) It will be the frame class that will be used for quick sort. Create any needed methods.

Step 2.   Make a copy of the public method version3QuickSort in SortArray.

Step 3.   Rename it to iterativeQuickSort().

Step 4.   Remove the call to the private recursive version3QuickSort(). It will be replaced with the iterative quick sort code. Do not remove the call to insertion sort.

Step 5.   Refer to the the Pre-Lab exercises and implement the code for the iterative simulation of recursive quick sort.

Checkpoint: Run CheckSort *with an array size of 500. Verify that iterative quick sort works correctly.*

Step 6. Change the value of the constant used to compute `quickSort100Ticks` to the value you found in Lab 9 (Advanced Sorts).

Step 7. Fill in the following table. Use the number of trials you used in the advanced sorting lab. Use 10 for the seed.

	RATIO FOR BASIC QUICKSORT	RATIO FOR ITERATIVE QUICKSORT
Size=100		
Size=200		
Size=300		
Size=400		
Size=500		
Size=600		
Size=700		
Size=800		
Size=900		
Size=1000		

Step 8. Plot the points for the ratios for quick sort and iterative quick sort on the following graph.

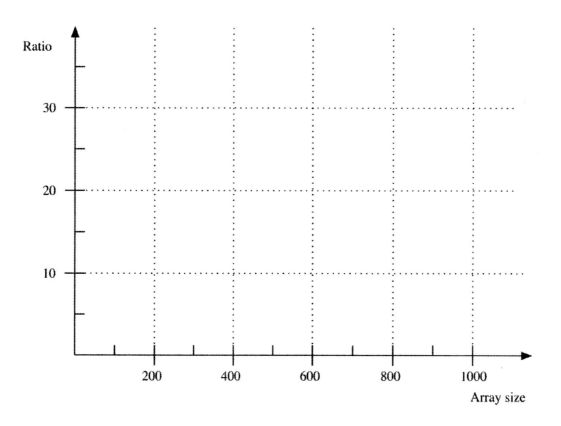

Animated Maze

All of the classes needed for the MazeApplication exist. This application is based on the AnimatedApplication framework. If you have not already, you should look at the description of it in Appendix A. The class that you will be working on is MazeActionThread. There is one other class that is specific to this application that you will need to work with. This class is Maze. Take a look at them now, if you have not done so already.

Step 1. Move the files maze1.txt through maze6.txt to the directory that your particular implementation of Java reads from and writes to.

Step 2. Compile the class MazeApplication. Run the main method in MazeApplication.

Checkpoint: If all has gone well, you should get a graphical user interface with step controls along the top and application setup controls on the bottom. There should be one text field where you can enter the name of a file containing the maze data. Type maze2.txt for the text file and then press enter. There should be a message indicating that it is now the maze input file. If not, check to make sure that you copied the file to the correct place. The application will read the maze. It should correspond, except for the start and goal, to the first maze from the Pre-Lab. The start should be at location (0,0). The goal should be at location (1,1). Enter 2 and 5 for the start. Press enter. The position of the start star should change. Enter 0 and 3 for the goal. Press enter. The position of the goal circles should change. Now the picture should match the Pre-Lab. Step twice. The application should finish.

Step 3. Create a new class named MazeFrame. Make it a private inner class in MazeActionThread. It will be the frame class that will be used to simulate the recursive search of the maze. Create any needed methods for the MazeFrame class.

Step 4. Refer to the exercises from the Pre-Lab and implement the code for the method searchMaze() in MazeActionThread. Don't forget to visit the goal when you find it.

Step 5. Code to create steps in the animation need to be added. Put the following line immediately after every call to visitSquare() or scheduleSquare().

```
animationPause();
```

Step 6. Call searchMaze() in the method executeApplication(). Set the variable goalFound with the value returned by the call.

Final Checkpoint: Run MazeApplication. Set up the application with maze2.txt. Use a start of (2,5). Use a goal of (0,3).

Step the application twice. A red dot should appear in the start square indicating that it was the most recently visited.

Step the application once more. A cyan circle should appear in one of the neighbors. This is a scheduled square. It should be the first one pushed on the stack.

Step the application twice more. The other two open squares next to the start should be filled with cyan circles, indicating that they have been scheduled.

Step the application once more. The last cyan dot should turn red as it is visited. The start will turn blue, which is the indication of a visited square that is not most recent.

Continue stepping the application. Eventually, the application should end with the red dot filling the center of the goal and a message will appear that it was found.

Run MazeApplication. Set up the application with maze2.txt. Use a start of (0,3). Use a goal of (0,7).

This time the application should search every square except goal. It will finish and the message should not appear.

Try the other mazes. Create ones of your own. Enjoy!

Post-Lab Follow-Ups

1. Develop and implement an iterative version of merge sort.

2. Suppose one wanted to keep the size of the stack as small as possible in the iterative version of quick sort. By comparing the sizes of the subranges, decide which half will be better for keeping the stack small. Implement this and print out the size of the stack. Compare this with the original version.

3. Modify the Maze application so it displays the path from the starting point to the current location in blue.

Lab 14   Queue Implementation and Client

Goal

In this lab you will work with queues. You will implement an event queue and then use it along with another queue in a simulation of customers waiting in a line at a bank.

Resources

- Chapter 23: Queue, Deque, and Priority Queues
- Chapter 24: Queue, Deque, and Priority Queue Implementations
- *QueueInterface.html*—API documentation for the queue ADT
- *PriorityQueueInterface.html*—API documentation for the priority queue ADT
- *SimulationEventQueueInterface.html*—API documentation for the event queue ADT
- *SimulationEventInterface.html*—API documentation for the events on the event queue ADT
- *Customer.html*—API documentation for a class representing a customer in a waiting line
- *BankLine.html*—API documentation for a class representing a line of customers in a bank
- *Report.html*—API documentation for a class representing a class that will display a report for the simulation
- *VectorQueue.java*—A sample implementation of Queue (in *QueuePackage*)
- *Bank.jar*—The final animated application
- *Lab14Graphs.pdf*—Printable versions of the graphs for this lab

Java Files

In directory Bank Simulation
- *Customer.java*
- *CustomerGenerator.java*
- *Teller.java*
- *BankLine.java*
- *Report.java*
- *BankApplication.java*
- *BankActionThread.java*
- There are other files used to animate the application. For a full description see Appendix A.

In directory QueuePackage
- *QueueInterface.java*
- *PriorityQueueInterface.java*
- *SimulationEventInterface.java*
- *SimulationEvent.java*
- *SimulationEventQueueInterface.java*

Introduction

A queue is a data structure that allows you to add items at the end and remove items from the front. It is a natural representation of a waiting line. A priority queue changes the add method. Instead of always adding at the end, it will insert the item into the queue according to a priority. The higher the priority, the closer to the front the item will be.

Event-Driven Simulations

One way of doing a simulation is to keep a list of all the events that have been scheduled to occur in the future. At each turn in the simulation, the event with the earliest time is removed from the list and processed. All of the events will be associated with an object. Processing the event will change the state of the object and may schedule new events to be processed at a later time. When designing a simulation, it will be important to have an idea of how the sequence of events flows in the system.

For example, consider a traffic light simulation where the light changes color every minute. What are the possible events in the simulation?
- The light turns green.
- The light turns red.
- The light turns yellow.
- A car arrives at the intersection.
- A car leaves the intersection.

Consider the traffic light first. What happens when the light turns red?

Event: Light turns red
    State change: The color of the light becomes red.
    Operations/Events to schedule: The light turns green in 60 seconds in the future.

Similarly, for the next two events,

Event: Light turns green
    State change: The color of the light becomes green.
    Operations/Events to schedule: The light turns yellow in 50 seconds in the future.

Event: Light turns yellow
    State change: The color of the light becomes yellow.
    Operations/Events to schedule: The light turns red in 10 seconds in the future.

Pictorially, the events for the light are

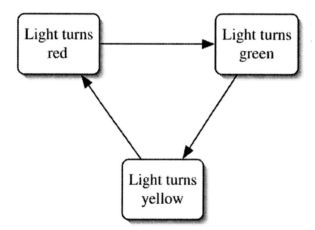

Now consider the events for the car. What happens when the car arrives at the light? It must check the color of the light to see if it can go through the intersection. If the light is red, the car will have to stop and wait. Can the car schedule when it will leave the intersection? No. Unlike with the light, the time that the car leaves has yet to be determined. There must be some place where the car will wait until it can be notified that it may continue. Once it receives notification, then it can schedule when it will leave the intersection.

Where will the car wait? The natural choice is a queue associated with the traffic light. What happens when the car arrives and the light is green? Can the car just go through the intersection? If there are cars waiting, a crash has just happened.

Event: Car arrives at the intersection
   State change: None for now (arrival time could be recorded though).
   Operations/Events to schedule: If the light is green and there are no cars waiting, schedule leaving the intersection 3 seconds in the future. Otherwise, put the car on the queue.

The question now is, "How do cars waiting at the light get going again?" Some event must trigger them. In this case, it will be when the light turns green. The design for that event must change.

Event: Light turns green (Version 2)
   State change: The color of the light beomes green.
   Operations/Events to schedule: The light turns yellow in 50 seconds. The light notifies the first car waiting in the queue that it can go now.

This takes care of the first car in the line, but what about the others? Each car in turn will notify the one behind it. This raises another question, "Can all the cars make it through the light in a single turn?" Sometimes the answer will be no. The time that the light is green will play a role. Clearly, all the cars cannot start at the same time but must be staggered. This indicates that the event queue must play a role. There must be another event.

Event: Waiting car checks intersection
   State change: None.
   Operations/Events to schedule: If the light is red or yellow, do nothing. Otherwise, schedule leave intersection 3 seconds in the future. Also, it will remove itself from the queue and notify the next car that it can check the intersection in 1 second.

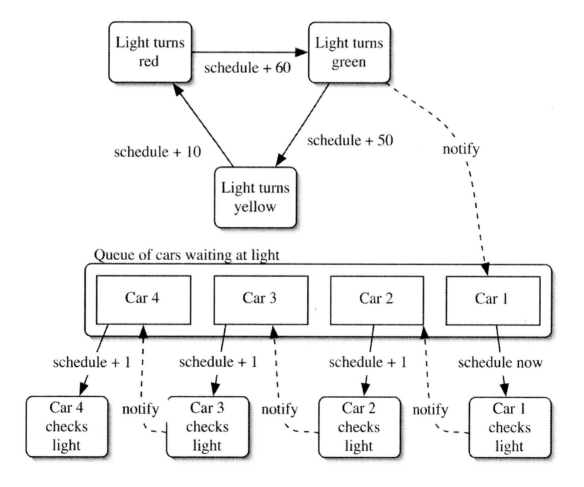

There is only one event left.

Event: Car leaves intersection
  State change: None for now (the time the car leaves the intersection could be recorded).
  Operations/Events to schedule: None.

One question is how do all the car arrival events get scheduled. One possibility is that they are all generated and placed on the event queue before the simulation starts. Another possibility is that there is a car generator object with a single event of its own.

Event: Generate Car
  State change: None.
  Operations/Events to schedule: Create a car and schedule it to enter the intersection now. Generate delta, a random time interval. Schedule a generate car event at time delta in the future.

This is similar to the operation of the traffic light except that the events occur at a random interval instead of a fixed one.

Events

Essentially, an event encapsulates a time and what to do at that time. They will support the interface in `SimulationEventInterface`. The four methods that must be supported are:

  getTime(): Get the time for the event.
  getDescription(): Get a string describing the event.
  getPostActionReport(): Get a string describing what the event did.
  process(): Do the actions required of the event.

The time and description of the event will be set when the event is created. The `process` method will be specialized for each particular event class. The last thing that `process` should do is to set a string, which the `getPostActionReport` method can return. Strictly speaking, the two methods that return the strings are not needed for the simulation, but they are useful in the animated application. The only really interesting method is `process()`.

To make it easier to create new events, the abstract class `SimulationEvent` has been created. It defines all of the methods, except for process, which is abstract. All a subclass needs to do is to have a constructor and a process method. An example of such a class is the inner class `GenerateCustomerEvent` in the `CustomerGenerator` class. Making the event class an inner class eases the coding marginally. The inner class will have access to all of the private variables of the class it is inside.

Pre-Lab Visualization

The Simulation Event Queue

The event queue is very similar to a priority queue. It has two major differences. The first difference is that the event queue acts as a timekeeper for the simulation. Every time an event is removed from the event queue, the simulation time moves forward to be the same as the time for the event that was just removed.

The second difference is that events that are before the current time of the event queue will not be added. If that were allowed, the arrow of time would not always go in the forward direction.

The major operation is the `add()` method. Suppose the following event is received by the add method.

```
┌──────────────┐
│   Event Z    │
│  Time: 15    │
└──────────────┘
```

In each of the following event queues, show where it would be added.

The Events   The current time: 10

```
┌────────────────────────────────────────────────────────────────┐
│  ┌──────────────┐                                                │
│  │   Event A    │                                                │
│  │  Time: 10    │                                                │
│  └──────────────┘                                                │
└────────────────────────────────────────────────────────────────┘
```

The Events   The current time: 10

```
┌────────────────────────────────────────────────────────────────┐
│                                                                  │
│                                                                  │
│                                                                  │
└────────────────────────────────────────────────────────────────┘
```

The Events   The current time: 10

```
┌────────────────────────────────────────────────────────────────┐
│  ┌──────────────┐  ┌──────────────┐  ┌──────────────┐            │
│  │   Event A    │  │   Event B    │  │   Event C    │            │
│  │  Time: 10    │  │  Time: 12    │  │  Time: 17    │            │
│  └──────────────┘  └──────────────┘  └──────────────┘            │
└────────────────────────────────────────────────────────────────┘
```

The Events   The current time: 10

```
┌────────────────────────────────────────────────────────────────┐
│  ┌──────────────┐  ┌──────────────┐  ┌──────────────┐            │
│  │   Event A    │  │   Event B    │  │   Event C    │            │
│  │  Time: 10    │  │  Time: 12    │  │  Time: 13    │            │
│  └──────────────┘  └──────────────┘  └──────────────┘            │
└────────────────────────────────────────────────────────────────┘
```

The Events   The current time: 15

```
┌────────────────────────────────────────────────────────────────┐
│  ┌──────────────┐  ┌──────────────┐                              │
│  │   Event D    │  │   Event E    │                              │
│  │  Time: 18    │  │  Time: 20    │                              │
│  └──────────────┘  └──────────────┘                              │
└────────────────────────────────────────────────────────────────┘
```

The Events   The current time: 15

| Event D
Time: 15 | Event E
Time: 15 | Event F
Time: 20 |

The Events   The current time: 17

| Event F
Time: 20 | Event G
Time: 22 |

Give an algorithm for inserting an event into an event queue.

Show the operation of the algorithm on the previous event queue examples.

Using an Event Queue in a Simulation

Suppose that the event queue is working. Some code is needed to drive the simulation forward. (It is called an event loop.)

When should the simulation stop?

At each step in the simulation, what must happen?

Given an algorithm for the event loop.

The Bank Line Simulation

In the lab, an event simulation will be created. It will simulate customers waiting to be served at a bank by tellers. Beside the animation and event classes, there will be five main classes that implement the bank simulation. Four of them will have associated animation displays. Pictorially, their relations are

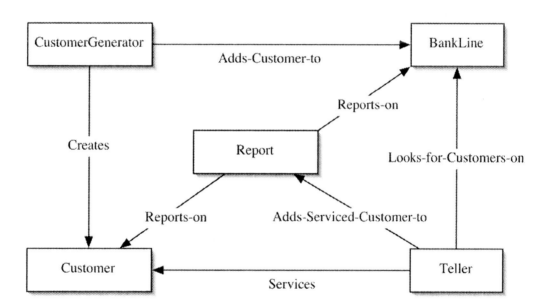

A customer in this simulation has very few responsibilities. The major responsibility of this class is to be able to draw a graphic representation of itself. When the customer is created, it will be given a name and the current time. At some time in the future it will be notified (by the teller) that it has been serviced. Once that has happened, it has the responsibility to be able to compute the time that it waited. The time it starts waiting and the time it is serviced will both be displayed. Consult *Customer.html* for names of the methods it implements.

The BankLine class is nearly as free of responsibilities as Customer. Besides its responsibilities as a queue, it has the additional responsibility of being able to draw itself.

The Report class has the responsibility for presenting the results of the simulation. It will produce two averages. The first is the average time that the customers currently in the line have waited. The second is the average time that the serviced customers waited. To accomplish the first task, the Report class will have access to the bank line. It will iterate over the customers in the line, requesting the time they started waiting. It will use these values to compute the average time waited. To satisfy the second requirement, it will keep a list of customers that have finished. It will iterate over them, requesting the time they waited. This places a requirement on Teller to give the customer to the Report object when the teller removes the customer from the bank line. The last requirement of Report is to display the current time of the simulation. This means that the simulation loop will need to inform the Report object of the current time after every step.

The CustomerGenerator class is one of the two classes that interact with the event queue. It has an event for customer generation.

Event: Generate Customer
State change: Customer name/count is updated.
Operations/Events to schedule: Create a new customer. Add the customer to the bank line. Schedule a generate customer event at a random time in the future.

The Teller class is the other class that interacts with the event queue. It will check the line for a customer to service.

What will happen if there is a customer in line?

What will happen if there isn't a customer in line?

Similar to generating a customer, the amount of time required to handle the customer will be random. The maximum time will be one of the parameters of the constructor. The other time used by the teller is the period between checking the line. Assuming that the tellers are very vigilant, the line will be checked every second.

Complete the event specification. (Teller has a method serve(), which encapsulates its responsibilities for serving the customer.)

Event: Check Bank Line for a Customer

 State change:

 Operations/Events to schedule:

Give an algorithm for the process method of the event.

Lab 14 Queue Implementation and Client

Directed Lab Work

Implementing the Event Queue

All but two of the classes needed in today's lab exist. The first class that will be worked on is the SimulationEventQueue.

Step 1.   In the QueuePackage, create a new class named SimulationEventQueue.

Step 2.   In the class declaration, make it implement SimulationEventQueueInterface.

Step 3.   Create method stubs for each of the methods in the interface.

Checkpoint: The class should compile now.

Step 4.   Create a private variable to store the current simulation time.

Step 5.   Create a private variable to store the contents of the queue.

Step 6.   Implement all of the methods except for add(). You may find the class VectorQueue helpful.

Step 7.   In the remove() method, add code to change the current time of the event queue.

Step 8.   Refer to the Pre-Lab exercises and implement the add() method.

Checkpoint: The class should compile.

The Bank Line Animation

Checkpoint: The bank application should run. At the very start of the set up phase init() will be called. The customer generator in its constructor puts its initial event on the event queue. That should show up as the next event. No customers should be in the line. Fred should be waiting patiently for customers to show up. The report should indicate that there are no customers waiting or served. The simulation time is 0.0.

At this point, it would be nice to see the event queue in operation. Code to drive the simulation will be added into the BankActionThread.

Creating the Event Loop

Step 9.   In the method executeApplication() in BankActionThread, add code that will repeatedly take events from the event queue and process them. Refer to the Pre-Lab exercises.

The display for the simulation has a few requirements for what happens in the event loop.

Step 10.   Inside the loop after the event has been processed, get the post action report from the event and use it to set lastEventReport.

Step 11.   If there is a next event, get the description and use it to set nextEventAction.

Step 12.   Update the time for the report.

Step 13.   The last code in the loop should be the line that will pause the animation.

```
animationPause();
```

Checkpoint: Compile and run the application. Press go. Customers should be generated and placed one at a time into the line. You should see them. Unfortunately, Fred is busy with his coffee. The simulation should stop once it hits 1000.

Completing the Teller Event

It is time for Fred to get to work. The process method for CheckForCustomerEvent inside the Teller class needs to be completed.

Step 14. Refer to the Pre-Lab exercises and complete the code for the method process().

Step 15. If no customer was served, set serving to null.

Step 16. At the end of processing, make sure to set postActionReport with a string describing the actions taken by the event.

Step 17. In the constructor for Teller, add code that will generate the first CheckForCustomerEvent. (This is similar to how the customer generator operates.)

Checkpoint: The teller should now take customers from the line. As customers are serviced, the report should change. Step and carefully trace the operation of the simulation. Verify that it is operating correctly.

Change the service interval time and verify that customers are handled quicker.

Graphing the Results

Step 18. Run the simulation with a maximum interval of 20 and a simulation time limit of 1000. Fill in the following table.

MAXIMUM SERVICE TIME	AVERAGE WAIT TIME FOR CUSTOMERS SERVED
6	
8	
10	
12	
14	
16	
18	
20	
22	
24	

Step 19.   Use the table to plot points on the following graph.

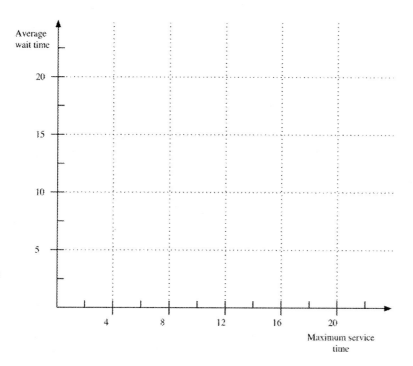

Suppose the service time is greater than the interval that customers appear. You expect that the teller will fall behind and the length of the line will increase without bound. If the service time is less, you expect that the teller will be able to keep up.

The interesting question is what happens when the service and interval times are the same. How long will the line be on average in this case? It turns out that the average, as the simulation time increases, will approach infinity. This will also have an effect on the average waiting time.

Step 20.   Run the application 20 times with the initial settings and record the average. (Warning: If you set the animation delay time to be too small, the animation may not stop at the end of the simulation but restart at time zero.)

Step 21.   What was the maximum average wait?

Step 22.   What was the minimum average wait?

Post-Lab Follow-Ups

1. Implement a new version of SimulationEventQueue, which uses a linked list.

2. Add two private queues to the CustomerGenerator that will store name syllables. When generating a name, take one syllable from each queue and concatenate them together. Put the syllables back on the ends of their respective queues. Set the queues so that each has a length that is a different prime.

3. Modify the simulation so that it has two tellers that take customers from a single line.

4. Modify the simulation so that it has two tellers, each with their own separate line.

5. Add an event to the Report class to collect statistics. Each time the event occurs, the length of the line will be recorded in order to compute the average, minimum, and maximum length of the line.

6. One of the good things about an event-driven simulation is that it will jump over times where nothing is happening. In the animation, this can cause sudden jumps in time. Add a class that will generate dummy events every second. The only responsibility of the event is to schedule the next dummy event.

7. *For those familiar with statistics and calculus:* Change the CustomerGenerator class so that the time between customers is determined according to a Gaussian distribution with a given mean and standard deviation. (To do this, consult a book on statistics and find a table that gives the cumulative distribution for a Gaussian distribution. Generate a value between 0 and 1 and interpolate to find a z score. From this, use the mean and standard deviation for the desired distribution to find your value.) Make a similar change for the service time for the Teller class. There are other distributions you can try as well.

8. Change the BankLine to be a priority queue. Each customer generated will have one of two priorities, high or low. Have the Report class report the average waiting time for each priority level.

9. *For those familiar with Java graphics:* Make the event queue a displayed object by the animation.

Lab 15   Tree Client

Goal

In this lab you will use a binary tree to create a Huffman code for compressing data.

Resources

- Chapter 25: Trees
- *TreeInterface.html*—API documentation for the tree ADT
- *BinaryTreeInterface.html*—API documentation for the binary tree ADT
- *HuffmanTreeInterface.html*—API documentation for the Huffman tree ADT
- *HuffmanTree.html*—API documentation for the class HuffmanTree
- *SymbolFrequencyPacket.html*—API documentation for the class SymbolFrequencyPacket, which is the data in a node of a Huffman tree
- *Message.html*—API documentation for the class Message, which is a buffer containing a message of type Character
- *Code.html*—API documentation for the class Code, which is a buffer containing the coded message
- *Encode.jar*—The working application

Java Files

Files in Directory *Huffman Code:*
- *FindDefaultDirectory.java*
- *EncodeApplication.java*
- *EncodeActionThread.java*
- *Code.java*
- *Message.java*
- There are other files used to animate the application. For a full description see Appendix A.

In TreePackage
- *SymbolFrequencyPacket.java*
- *TreeInterface.java*
- *BinaryTreeInterface.java*
- *HuffmanTreeInterface.java*
- *HuffmanTree.java*
- There are other files in tree package, but they will not be used in this lab.

Input Files

- *message1.txt*—A two line message to encode
- *message2.txt*—The same message as the first, but spaces have been added
- *message3.txt*—A four line message to encode
- *message4.txt*—A longer message to encode

Introduction

A tree is a data structure that has a lot of different uses. Today's lab will focus on using a tree to create a variable length code for an alphabet.

Using a Tree to Represent a Code

Consider a binary tree where each leaf holds a different symbol. The path from the root of the tree to each symbol is unique. These paths can be used as binary codes for the symbols. Each right branch is a one, and each left branch is a zero. The following tree is an example.

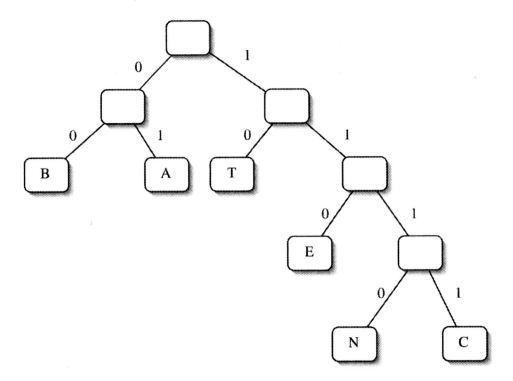

It corresponds to the following binary code:

SYMBOL	CODE
A	01
B	00
C	1111
E	110
N	1110
T	10

Codes that are based on trees will have the prefix property. This means that no code is the prefix of any other code. If this is not the case, decoding is more difficult. For example, suppose that the symbol Y was given the code 11. If the coded message is 110111..., what does the initial 11 represent? Is it a Y? Or is it the start of E, N, or C?

Once a tree for a code has been generated, it can be used for both encoding and decoding. To encode a character, just follow the branches from the root to the desired symbol. At each branch, output a 1 or 0. To decode a message, start at the root. For each 0, take a left branch. For each 1, take a right branch. When a leaf is reached, output the symbol and start over at the top.

Pre-Lab Visualization

Huffman Encoding

A Huffman code is a variable length code that minimizes the length of the message. The basic idea is that symbols that are frequently encountered in the message will be represented by short codes. On the other hand, infrequent symbols will have longer codes. The following tree was constructed from the message:

THE CAT IS THAT CAT

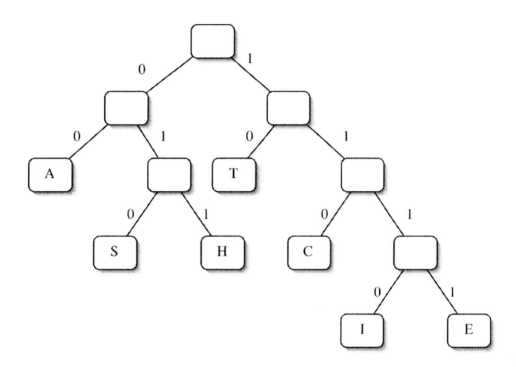

Encode the message: THE CAT IS THAT CAT

How many bits were used?

If each character had a fixed length (each of the 7 symbols can be represented using a 3-bit code), how many bits would be used?

Getting the Frequencies

The structure of the Huffman tree must depend on the frequencies of the letters. Therefore, the first task is to compile a count of each letter in the message. Consider the following message:

CHEESES CHEESES
T CLEESE SELLS THE CHEESES

How many times does each character appear in the message?

SYMBOL	COUNT
A	
C	
E	
H	
S	
T	

To construct the counts, you can start with an array of size 128. This is large enough to hold a count for each of the 128 possible 7-bit ASCII characters. (Any character with an integer value greater than 128 is ignored.)

Give an algorithm for computing the frequency count for the letters in a message. The message will be stored in an object of type Message. It obeys the Java Iterator interface, so you can use it in that fashion to get the characters one at a time. Review its protocol before you start. Assume that there is a method charToInt, which will return the ASCII integer value associated with a given character.

Creating the Initial Forest of Trees

Once the counts have been done, the next step is to create a collection (forest) of Huffman trees. To start there will be one tree for each possible symbol. Each of the trees will have a single node, where the data portion is an instance of SymbolFrequencyPacket. The packet's list will contain just the character. The packet's frequency will be the count for that character.

Fill in the initial trees for the characters and counts that were found in the previous section.

Forest of Huffman trees

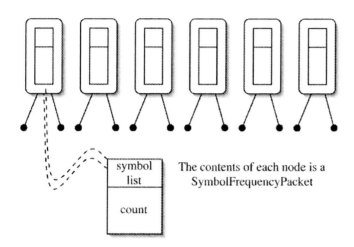

symbol
list

count

The contents of each node is a
SymbolFrequencyPacket

Give an algorithm for creating the forest of trees given an array of the counts. Review the protocol for SymbolFrequencyPacket and HuffmanTree before hand. Assume that there is a method intToChar, which will return the character associated with a given ASCII integer code value.

Finding the Code Tree

At this point an iterative process will be applied to construct a single Huffman tree out of the forest of trees. It will be illustrated by a small example. At each step the two trees with the smallest frequency will be removed from the forest and replaced by a single tree. The new tree will have the tree with the smallest frequency on the left and the second smallest tree will be on the right. The list of symbols in the root will be the concatenation of the lists from the two smallest trees. The frequency in the root will be the sum of the frequencies of the two smaller trees.

In the following example, the two smallest trees in the forest are the Z and the X.

Initial forest of Huffman trees

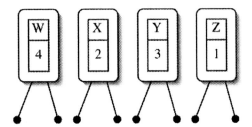

Those two trees will be removed and then used to form the tree that will be added. Since the count for Z is less than that of X, Z will go on the left. (This is an arbitrary choice that will make no difference in the effectiveness of the code, but it can make it easier to check that the construction process is working properly.)

Forest of Huffman trees after combining X and Z

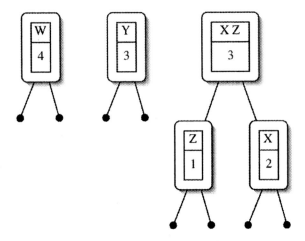

Now the two smallest trees are the Y and XZ, both with a count of 3. Which one should go on the left? Pick either one. If you need to pick among a number of trees of the same frequency, any one of them can be safely chosen.

Forest of Huffman trees after combining X Z and Y

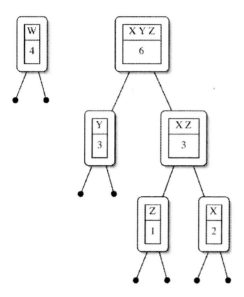

The final step is to combine the last two trees in the forest.

Final forest of Huffman trees

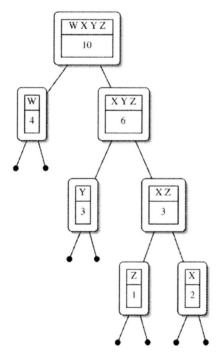

Show the trees combined at each step and the final Huffman tree resulting from the initial forest that was constructed in the previous section. If it is correct, the message 111011110101100 will either decode to CHEST or HCEST.

Trees combined in step 1:

Trees combined in step 2:

Trees combined in step 3:

Trees combined in step 4:

Trees combined in step 5:

Final tree:

Give an algorithm for creating the forest of trees given an array of the counts. Assume that the forest of trees is stored in an array. **Hint**: It might be helpful to swap the tree of smallest frequency with the last tree in the array.

Encoding the Message

Encode the message

CHEESE

using the final Huffman tree from the previous section.

Give an algorithm for encoding a single character. The coded text will be stored in an object of type Code. It is a displayed object of the animation. As the bits are added to the code, they will show up in color on the animation panel. The HuffmanTree class is also a displayed object. As the final tree is accessed, the path of nodes from the root is highlighted. Don't forget to review the protocol for both classes before starting.

Give an algorithm for encoding a message. The message is stored in an object of type Message. It is a displayed object. As each character is accessed, it will change color.

Directed Lab Work

Getting the Frequencies

All of the classes needed for the EncodeApplication exist. This application is based on the AnimatedApplication framework. If you have not already, you should look at the description of it in Appendix A. The class that you will be working on is EncodeActionThread. There are a number of other classes that are specific to this application that you will need to work with. These classes are SymbolFrequencyPacket, HuffmanTree, Message, and Code. Take a look at them now, if you have not done so already.

Step 1. Move the files *message1.txt* through *message4.txt* to the directory your particular implementation of Java reads from and writes to.

Step 2. Compile the class EncodeApplication. Run the main method in EncodeApplication.

Checkpoint: If all has gone well, you should get a graphical user interface with step controls along the top and application setup controls on the bottom. There should be one text field where you can enter the name of a file containing the message to encode. Type message2.txt for the text file and then press enter. There should be a message indicating that it is now the text file. If not, check to make sure that you copied the file to the correct place. The application will read the text into Message. Step twice. The first two lines of the message should appear with the first character displayed in red.

Step 3. In EncodeActionThread, add a declaration for an array of integers that will hold the counts.

Step 4. In the method getCounts() in EncodeActionThread, add code that will get the characters from the message one by one and compute and return an array with the frequencies. Use the existing method charToInt() in EncodeActionThread. Note that it expects a char and will return an Integer. Refer to the algorithm from the Pre-Lab exercises.

Step 5. In the executeAppliction() method, call getCounts() and then print the array that is returned.

Checkpoint: The application should run. Use message1.txt for the text file. Step twice. The counts array should be printed on the system output. It should match the counts from the Pre-Lab exercises. The message should also show that it is on the last line and no characters in the message should be red.

Now that the counts are ready, it is time to create the forest of trees.

Creating the Initial Forest of Trees

Step 6. In the method getInitialTrees() in EncodeActionThread, add code that will use the frequencies array to create one Huffman tree for each nonzero count. Use the existing method intToChar() in EncodeActionThread. Note that it expects an int and will return a Character. Refer to the algorithm from the Pre-Lab exercises.

Step 7. In the executeAppliction() method, call getInitialTrees().

Step 8. Set the variable numberOfTrees.

Step 9. After setting numberOfTrees, add in the following line of code to make the animation pause. (For further questions, see the discussion in Appendix A.)

```
animationPause();
```

Checkpoint: The application should run. Use message1.txt *for the text file. Step twice. The initial forest of trees should be displayed.*

Finding the Code Tree

Step 10.   In the method combineTrees() in EncodeActionThread, add code that will combine the two smallest frequencies trees into a single tree in the forest. Refer to the algorithm from the Pre-Lab exercises.

Step 11.   At the end of the combineTrees() method, add in the following line of code to make the animation pause.

```
animationPause();
```

Step 12.   In the executeAppliction() method, call combineTrees().

Checkpoint: The application should run. Use message1.txt *for the text file. Step twice. The initial forest of trees should be displayed. Step once more. The T and the L should be combined into a single tree. The top of that tree should display a red 5.*

Step 13.   In the executeAppliction() method, revise the code so that trees are combined until the final code tree is the only one left. It should be at index 0.

Step 14.   After the final tree has been created, set the variable treeCreated to true.

Checkpoint: The application should run. Use message1.txt *for the text file. Step twice. The initial forest of trees should be displayed. Continue stepping. The sequence of forests should match those from the Pre-Lab exercises.*

Encoding the Message

Step 15.   In the method encodeCharacter() in EncodeActionThread, add code that will get a character from the message, encode it, and add a "0" or "1" depending for each left or right branch, respectively, that was taken. Refer to the Pre-Lab exercise.

Step 16.   After a character is added to the code, do an animation pause.

Step 17.   In the executeAppliction() method, get a character from the message.

Step 18.   After getting the character, reset the code tree.

Step 19.   After that, add code to make the animation pause.

Step 20.   Finally, call encodeCharacter().

Checkpoint: The application should run. Use message1.txt *for the text file. Step until the final code tree is displayed. Step once more. The first character in the message should be red. A "1" should appear in red in the code. The 22 (frequency of the right child of the root) of the code tree should appear in red to indicate the right branch was taken. Continue stepping and verify that the correct code is produced.*

Step 21.   In the executeAppliction() method, revise the code so each character in the message is encoded.

Step 22.   Print the final code buffer to System.out.

Final checkpoint: The application should run. Use message1.txt *for the text file. Each character in the message should be coded. Verify the code of the first part of the message "CHEESE" against the Pre-Lab results.*

Run the application for message2, message3, *and* message4. *Record the final code tree for each on paper. Decode the results by hand and verify the results.*

The trees for these texts may appear a bit strange since the space character does not draw. When highlighted, it will not show up either.

The tree for message4 *will have nodes that overlap each other towards the bottom. This can be alleviated a bit by having the application use a bigger window. (Change the value of DISPLAY_WIDTH to be larger.) Since there are 10 levels to the tree, this will only be a minor improvement.*

Post-Lab Follow-Ups

1. Develop and implement a method that uses a Dictionary to count the characters in a message.

2. Make a new version of the EncodeApplication that considers each word in the text as a symbol.

3. Make a new version of the EncodeApplication that strips any nonalphanumeric character from the message.

4. Modify the code to use a List instead of an array to hold the forest of Huffman trees. Use an iterator to find and remove the two smallest frequency trees.

5. Develop a format for representing a Huffman tree using a string of characters which is suitable to be written to a file. Add two methods to HuffmanTree. The method writeTree() will return a string that is the representation of the tree. The static method parseTree(String) will return a HuffmanTree equivalent to the representation in the String. Throw an exception if the string is not in the correct format. You might find it convenient to have some pattern of characters that marks the beginning and end of the representation as well.

6. Develop and implement a method that will decode a message using a HuffmanTree.

7. Create a new animated application that will read a Huffman tree from a file (Use the results from question 5.). Then read a message from another file and decode it. The Message and Code classes will require only minor changes.

8. Develop and implement an application that will read a fully parenthesized arithmetic expression with the binary operators +, *, -, /, and integer constants and display the expression tree. Use a recursive algorithm to evaluate the expression.

9. Use the classes from the previous problem and create an animated application. Step with each completed evaluation. Show the result in the node in red.

10. *For those familiar with Java graphics:* Change the drawOn method of HuffmanTree to make the displayed structure of the tree esthetically pleasing while having no overlapping nodes. There are a number of things you can try. For example, you can evenly space the nodes on every level, or you can stagger the nodes in a level vertically. Nodes on the same level do not have to be at the same height in the drawing. About the only requirement is that right and left links should be distinguishable from one another.

Lab 16   Tree Implementation

Goal

In this lab you will modify a binary tree so that its nodes have parent references. Post-order traversal will be implemented using the parent references.

Resources

- Chapter 25: Trees
- Chapter 26: Tree Implementations
- *TreeInterface.html*—API documentation for the tree ADT
- *BinaryTreeInterface.html*—API documentation for the binary tree ADT
- *BinaryTreeAccessInterface.html*—API documentation for a binary tree with an embedded current node
- *BinaryWithParentsTreeAccessInterface.html*—API documentation for a binary tree with an embedded current node that supports moving to the parent

Java Files

- *TestBinaryTree.java*
- *TestBasicAccess.java*
- *TestParentAccess.java*
- *TestPostorderIterator.java*
- *PreToPost.java*

In TreePackage
- *BinaryNode.java*
- *BinaryTree.java*
- *TreeInterface.java*
- *BinaryTreeInterface.java*
- *BinaryTreeAccessInterface.java*
- *BinaryWithParentsTreeAccessInterface.java*

Introduction

Binary Tree

A binary tree is a tree where every node has zero, one, or two children. Each node will have two links, one for each child. If the there is no child, the link will be null. The following is an example of a binary tree.

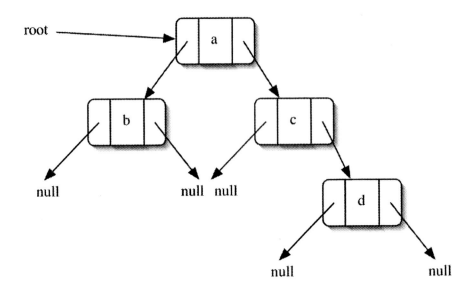

To travel in the tree, you must start at the root and traverse either right or left links until you reach the desired node. Just as a chain can be doubly linked to make it easier to move backward, you can add parent references to the nodes. Adding parent references to the preceding tree yields the following tree.

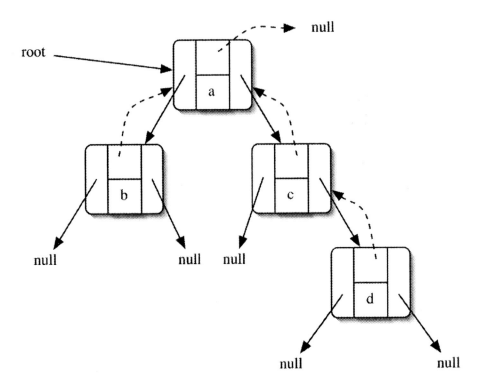

Constructing a Binary Tree

There is one detail about the implementation of BinaryTree that is important to understand for this lab. Consider the following chunk of code.

```
BinaryTree b1 = new BinaryTree("a");
BinaryTree b2 = new BinaryTree("b);
BinaryTree b3 = new BinaryTree("c", b1, b2);
BinaryTree b4 = new BinaryTree("d", b3, b3);
```

Make a prediction of the contents and structure of each tree at the end of the code.

b1   **b2**   **b3**   **b3**

The first two statements each create a tree containing one node. In the following trees, null references out of a node are not drawn.

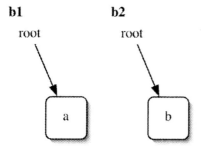

The third statement does not necessarily do what one might expect. The nodes from the two trees b1 and b2 are used to build the tree b3. It might not be expected that b1 and b2 no longer have access to those trees, but it is important for the integrity of b3.

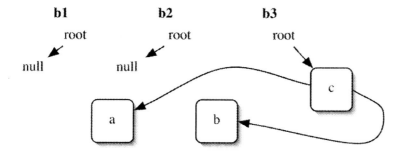

The final statement is requesting b3 twice. Since both subtrees cannot share the nodes, a copy must be made. The final picture is

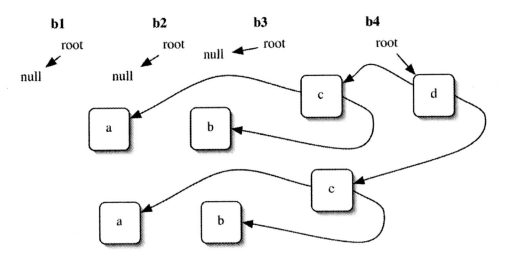

Basic Access to a Binary Tree

As defined in the class BinaryTree, there is not much you can do with the binary tree except to build and traverse it. For this lab an interface BinaryTreeAccessInterface has been defined that will allow a client the ability to move through the tree. This is similar to the DecisionTreeInterface, which was defined in Chapter 25.

There is a current reference, which is kept by the binary tree. It can be reset to the root of the tree. Query methods are provided to allow the client to ask if the current node has right or left children. There are methods that allow the client to move the current reference to the right or left child. Finally, there is a method that will allow the client to get the data in the node that is the current reference.

There are two fundamental questions that must be answered for the access.

> **What happens if the reference is advanced but the child does not exist?**
> **What happens if the tree is empty?**

One possibility is for the bad advance to throw an exception. Another possibility is to leave the reference where it is. A third possibility is to let the reference become null. All three are reasonable choices. In this implementation, the third option is chosen.

Once the current access becomes null, it should not be used. If the client asks for data, just return null. If the client attempts to move, leave it null. If the tree is empty, the current access will be null and it will behave in a reasonable way.

Once parent references have been added to the tree, the access interface will be extended with a query and move method that will work with the parent reference.

Parent References

For the most part, adding parent references to a binary tree is a simple operation. There are only two places where a parent reference will need to be changed. The first is privateSetTree() in BinaryTree. It is the place where two trees are composed together to create a larger tree. The parent references of the roots of the two subtrees must be fixed to point to the new root. The other place where parent references must be fixed is not as obvious.

Consider the copy operation from BinaryNode. It will make a copy of the top node, then recursively copy the subtrees. Note that the links cannot just be copied. If they were, they would point to the original nodes. Suppose that the following tree is going to be copied.

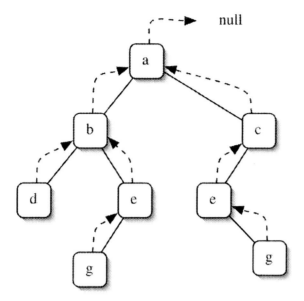

It will be assumed that copies of the subtrees will be made recursively. Once this is done, it just remains to link up the subtrees with a copy of the root node. The following picture shows the state of the copy at that point.

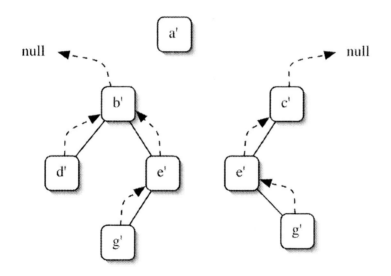

Show the links that must be formed. In the lab, a second version of the copy operation will be created that takes a single parameter, which will be the parent of the copy.

Post-Order Iterator

The strategy employed by the iterator is to keep a reference to the node that will be produced by the next method. When next is called, the value to be returned is retrieved from the referenced node. Then the reference will be moved to the next node.

In the following tree, label the nodes numerically with the order that they will be visited by a post-order traversal.

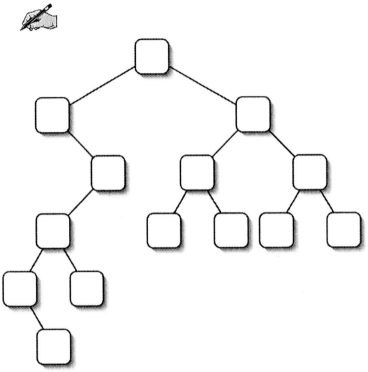

Constructor:
The constructor for the post-order iterator must find the first node in a post-order traversal. Give an algorithm for that operation.

HasNext():
This method is nearly trivial. What is the condition for hasNext() to return true?

Next():
The method next() must move to the next node in the post-order traversal. Examine the preceding tree and answer the following questions.

Can the next node ever be below the current node?

Is the next node ever not the parent of the current node?

How can those cases be recognized? Write down a condition.

If the next node is not the parent, give an algorithm for finding it.

Pre-Order Expressions

One way to construct an arithmetic expression is to use a prefix notation. The operations come before the arguments they will be applied to. Let's look at the problem of constructing an binary tree from a prefix expression. Consider the prefix expressions

```
*   +   1   /   2   3   -   4   5
+   1   +   +   3   4   5
-   +   3   4   /   2   +   3   4
```

Draw a binary tree for each of the expressions where the leaf nodes are values and the interior nodes are binary operations. A pre-order traversal must produce the prefix expression.

In the preceding prefix expressions; circle the tokens (values and operators) that are in the left subtree. Circle the tokens in the right subtree. This hints that a recursive algorithm can be used to construct the binary tree from the prefix expression.

Give a recursive design for getTree that constructs a binary tree from an expression.

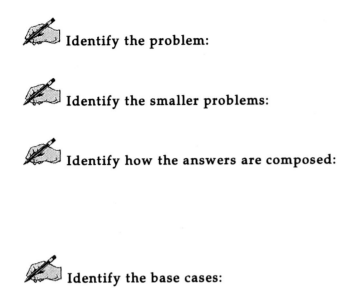 Identify the problem:

Identify the smaller problems:

Identify how the answers are composed:

Identify the base cases:

Compose the recursive definition:

Show the operation of your definition on the expression
* + 1 / 2 3 - 4 5

Directed Lab Work

The main classes that you will be working with today are BinaryTree and BinaryNode. Take a look at them now, if you have not done so already. To verify that these classes work, you can run TestBinaryTree.

Modifying BinaryTree for BasicAccess

Step 1.   Change the declaration of the BinaryTree so that it implements BinaryTreeAccessInterface.

Step 2.   In BinaryTree, add the six methods required by BinaryTreeAccessInterface.

Step 3.   In BinaryTree, add a private variable of type BinaryNode<T> that will reference the current access node.

Step 4.   Implement the each of the methods just added. Refer to the Pre-Lab.

Step 5.   Anytime the structure of the binary tree is changed, the access needs to be reset. Call resetAccess() in the constructors, setTree(), and clear().

Checkpoint: Compile BinaryNode and BinaryTree. Run TestBinaryTree and TestBasicAccess. All tests should pass.

Modifying BinaryTree with Parent References

Step 6.   In the class BinaryNode, add a private variable that will hold the parent reference.

Step 7.   Add a new constructor, which has four arguments: data, left, right, and parent.

Step 8.   Modify the constructor that takes three arguments to use the new constructor.

Step 9.   Create and fully implement three new methods in BinaryNode:
```
    public BinaryNodeInterface<T> getParent()
    public void setParent(BinaryNodeInterface<T> p)
    public boolean hasParent()
```

Checkpoint: Compile BinaryNode and BinaryTree. All tests in TestBinaryTree and TestBasicAccess should still pass.

Step 10.   Make a duplicate of the method copy() in BinaryNode and add a single argument BinaryNode<T> p to the duplicate.

Step 11.   In the duplicate, set the parent of newRoot to be p.

Step 12. In the original, set the parent of newRoot to be parent. (We will assume that if the original version of the copy method is being called, it is the top of the tree being copied and the parent should be the same as the node being copied. The duplicate version of copy will be used for all other nodes in the copy.)

Step 13. In both the original and the duplicate, change the two recursive calls to copy() so that they pass newRoot as the parameter.

Checkpoint: BinaryNode should compile successfully.

Checkpoint: Compile BinaryNode and BinaryTree. All tests in TestBinaryTree and TestBasicAccess should still pass.

The modification of BinaryNode is finished. The next goal is to modify BinaryTree appropriately. Any time a new binary tree is created, parent references for children may need to be set.

Step 14. Anywhere in BinaryTree that a left or right child is set, set a parent reference in an appropriate fashion. Since BinaryNodeInterface<T> does not have the methods for accessing the parent, a cast to BinaryNode<T> will be required.

Checkpoint: Compile BinaryNode and BinaryTree. All tests in TestBinaryTree and TestBasicAccess should still pass.

It is now time to add in the methods that will allow a client to move the current access to follow a parent reference.

Step 15. Change the declaration of the BinaryTree so that it implements BinaryWithParentsTreeAccessInterface.

Step 16. Add and implement the methods required by the interface.

Checkpoint: Compile BinaryNode and BinaryTree. All tests in TestBinaryTree and TestBasicAccess should still pass.

It is now time to see if the changes to BinaryNode and BinaryTree have really worked. All tests in TestParentAccess should pass.

Implementing a Post-Order Iterator with Parent References

Step 17. In the class BinaryTree, create a copy of the private inner class InorderIterator. Rename the copy to PostorderIterator.

Step 18. Keep the code in the methods for future reference. The private variable currentNode will be kept, but nodeStack will be deleted.

Step 19. Refer to the Pre-Lab exercises and create a method in PostorderIterator that will move the current node to the first node to be printed in a post-order traversal.

Step 20. Call the new method in the constructor just after setting the currentNode to the root.

Step 21. Complete the hasNext() method.

Step 22. Refer to the Pre-Lab exercises and complete the next() method. Don't forget to throw NoSuchElementException when there are no more elements to be iterated over.

Step 23. Remove nodeStack from PostorderIterator.

Step 24. Change the method getPostorderIterartor() so that it returns a new PostorderIterator instead of throwing an exception.

Checkpoint: Compile BinaryTree. All previous test code should still pass. All tests in TestPostorderIterator should pass.

Now that BinaryTree has a post-order iterator using parent references, it will be used to produce a post-order traversal of a binary expression tree.

Converting Prefix Expressions to Postfix

Step 25. The application PreToPost exists but needs to be completed.

*Checkpoint: The application should run. Enter the prefix expression * 3 4. The application will read the expression, then quit.*

Step 26. In the main, create a new Scanner that will break up the string that was read into tokens. Use next() to get the tokens as strings.

Step 27. Complete the method getTree() in PreToPost. Refer to the recursive design in the Pre-Lab exercises.

Step 28. Call the method getTree() in main to create the binary expression tree.

Step 29. Create a post-order iterator for the expression tree.

Step 30. Use the iterator to print out the values in the expression tree.

*Final checkpoint: The application should run. Enter the prefix expression * 3 4. The result should be 3 4 *.*

Run the application again. Enter the prefix expression - - / 4 3 + 8 7 2. The result should be 4 3 / 8 7 + - 2 -.

Test the application for other inputs. Try expressions that have too many or too few tokens.

Post-Lab Follow-Ups

1. Change the access interface so that it will throw an exception if there is no data value to return. Also change it so that if the client attempts to move to an empty child another exception is thrown. Modify `BinaryNode` and `BinaryTree` to satisfy the new access methods. Modify the `TestBasicAccess` and `TestParent` to test for the exceptions.

2. Use the parent references along with checking the direction of backtracking (determine if the current node is the left or right child of the parent) to implement the in-order iterator.

3. Use the parent references along with checking the direction of backtracking to implement the pre-order iterator.

4. Another way that the iterators can be implemented is to mark the nodes that have been visited by the iterator. This will require an extra variable stored in the node to indicate the marking. One problem with this implementation is that there can only be one iterator at a time. Use the parent references along with marking to implement the post-order iterator. Change `BinaryTree` so that there is a single instance of the iterator which is returned by the `getPostorderIterator()` method.

5. Use the parent references along with marking to implement the in-order iterator.

6. Use the parent references along with marking to implement the pre-order iterator.

7. Modify the application to use a string tokenizer to break up the arithmetic expressions using spaces and the four operators as delimeters.

8. Develop and implement a recursive method that will evaluate a binary expression tree.

9. Modify the application to work with Boolean expressions that use the binary operators ^ (and) and v (or) and the unary operator ~ (not).

Lab 17   Binary Search Tree Implementation

Goal

In this lab you will modify a binary search tree so that the nodes are threaded in order. In-order traversal will be implemented using the thread. A client using a binary search tree will be developed.

Resources

- Chapter 25: Trees
- Chapter 26: Tree Implementations
- Chapter 27: A Binary Search Tree Implementation
- *TreeInterface.html*—API documentation for the tree ADT
- *BinaryTreeInterface.html*—API documentation for the binary tree ADT
- *SearchTreeInterface.html*—API documentation for the binary search tree ADT

Java Files

- *TestBinaryTree.java*
- *TestBST.java*
- *Identifiers.java*

In TreePackage
- *BinaryNode.java*
- *BinaryTree.java*
- *BinarySearchTree.java*
- *TreeInterface.java*
- *BinaryTreeInterface.java*
- *SearchTreeInterface.java*

Input Files

- *Small.java*
- *X.java*

Introduction

Threaded Binary Trees

A binary tree is a tree where every node has zero, one, or two children. Each node will have two links, one for each child. In a threaded tree, an extra link is added that threads (links) all of the nodes in some fashion. In this lab, the threading will link the nodes according to an in-order traversal. In the following picture, the dashed lines indicate the thread links.

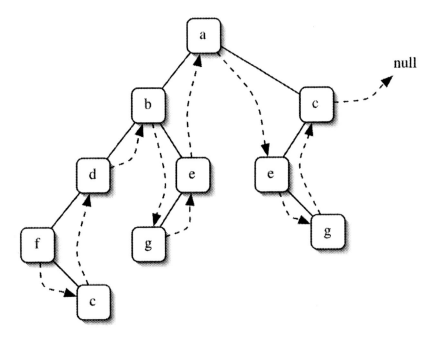

The first node in the thread is the first node in an in-order traversal.

Binary Search Tree

In a binary search tree, the values stored in the nodes cannot be arbitrary but must be orderable. The search tree property requires that all values in the left subtree must be less than the value stored in the node. Similarly, all values in the right subtree must be greater than the value stored in the node. A binary search tree must satisfy this property at all of its nodes. The following tree is a binary search tree with the same structure as the previous threaded tree.

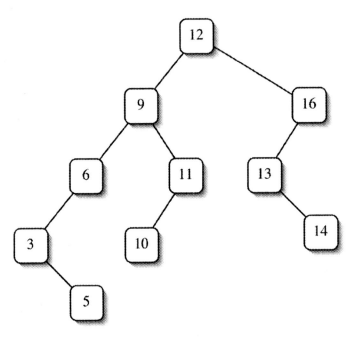

Examining each node, you see that the search tree property holds. For example, the values to the left of 9 are 3, 5, and 6, while the values to the right are 10 and 11. If any two values in this search tree are switched, it no longer satisfies the search tree property.

Notice that if the threads from the previous picture are followed, the values traversed will be in ascending order.

One nice property of a search tree is that adding a value in the tree will always be done at a leaf position.

Pre-Lab Visualization

BinaryNode Copy with Threads

One of the responsibilities of the binary node class is to make a copy of the tree rooted by the node. This is done recursively. The threads add a complication. Consider the following binary tree with threads.

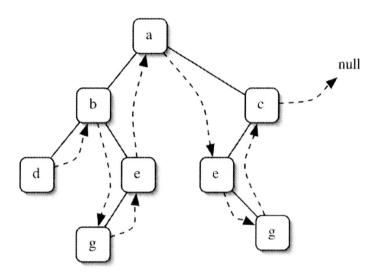

In making a copy, a new node is created for copying the root, and then the left and right subtrees are copied. Notice that the links cannot be a straight copy. If so, they would refer to nodes in the original. Assume that the recursive copy correctly threads all of the nodes within the subtree, with the exception of the last node. Here is a picture after the copies have been made.

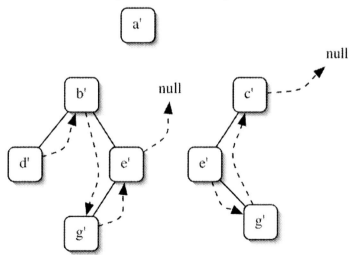

On the picture, indicate the changes that need to be made to complete the copy.

Give an algorithm for a method `linkSubtreeThreadOut(BinaryNode linkTo)` that will link the thread coming out of the left subtree.

Give an algorithm for a method `getSubtreeLeftmost()` that returns the node in the right subtree that should be the target of the thread from the root.

Use the previous two algorithms to show how the following tree is copied.

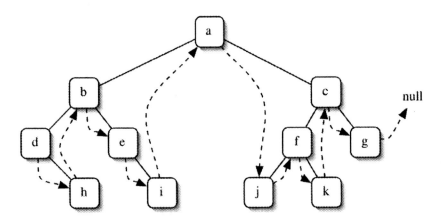

Lab 17   Binary Search Tree Implementation

In-Order Iterator

The in-order iterator for the threaded binary search tree is nearly trivial. It just needs to follow the thread links. It will have a current node. When the `next` method is invoked, the value in the current node will be returned.

What is the condition for `hasNext()` to return true?

What does the iterator do for `next()`?

The only minor complication is how the iterator is initialized. It must set the current node to the first node in the thread.

Give an algorithm for finding the first node in the thread.

Threading BinarySearchTree-Add

As nodes are added to the binary search tree, the threads will need to be adjusted.

Consider the following threaded initial binary search tree.

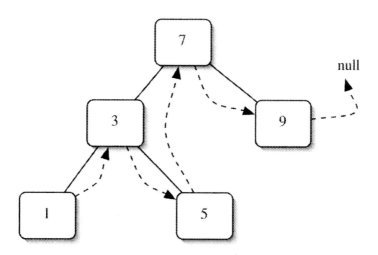

Adding the value 0 will result in the following tree. Put in the thread links and mark the ones that have changed. (Remember that the thread links give an in-order traversal of the tree.)

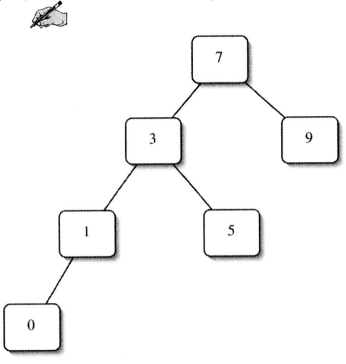

Adding the value 4 to the initial tree will result in the following tree. Put in the thread links and mark the ones that have changed.

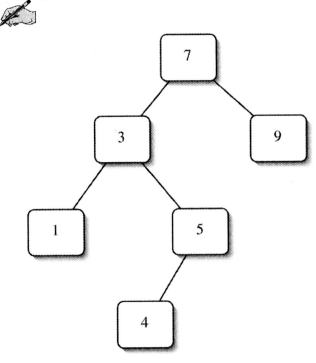

Adding the value 8 to the initial tree will result in the following tree. Put in the thread links and mark the ones that have changed.

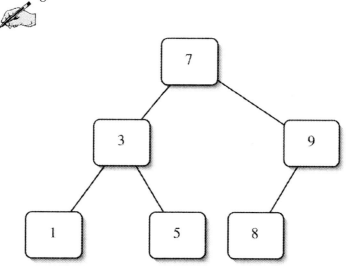

Adding the value 7.5 to the previous tree will result in the following tree. Put in the thread links and mark the ones that have changed.

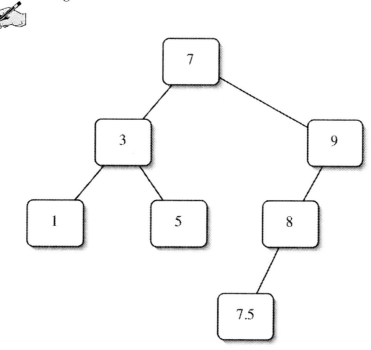

All of the previous examples added the node as a left child. If the insertion is on the left, where must the thread for the inserted value go?

If the insertion is on the left, where is the thread that must be changed to refer to the new node?

Give an algorithm for finding the node with the thread to change. (You may assume that the tree has parent references and use them in the algorithm.)

Adding the value 2 to the initial tree will result in the following tree. Put in the thread links and mark the ones that have changed.

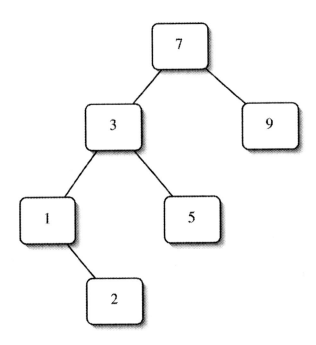

Adding the value 6 to the initial tree will result in the following tree. Put in the thread links and mark the ones that have changed.

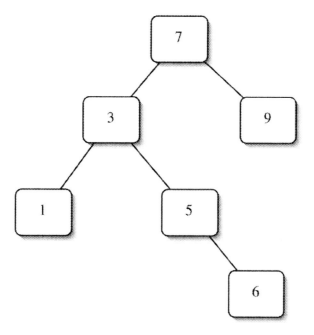

Adding the value 10 to the initial tree will result in the following tree. Put in the thread links and mark the ones that have changed.

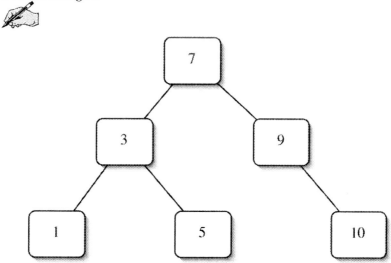

If the insertion is on the right, where must the thread for the inserted value go?

If the insertion is on the right, where is the thread that must be changed to refer to the new node?

Threading BinarySearchTree—Remove

Examine the code for remove in `BinarySearchTree.java`. There are three cases for remove. If the node to be removed has no children, it is just removed. If the node to be removed has one child, its child is moved up in the tree. If the node to be removed has two children, its in-order predecessor's data value is copied up. The predecessor is then removed.

The only changes to the structure of tree will involve a node with zero or one children.

Consider the following trees. The node that will be removed is indicated with an X. Draw the threads and mark the node whose thread will no longer have a target when X is removed.

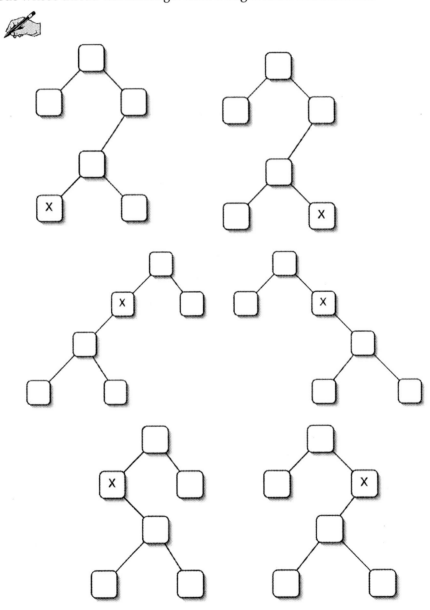

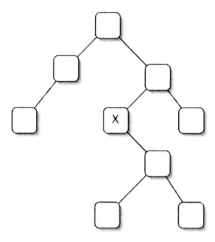

The change will always be for the in-order predecessor of the node to be removed. Surprisingly, if the node has no in-order predecessor within the search tree, nothing needs to be done.

Depending on the structure of the tree, there are two cases for finding the in-order predecessor of a node. Identify the cases and give an algorithm for each one.

Case1:

Case 2:

Directed Lab Work

The main classes that you will be working with today are a couple old friends `BinaryTree` and `BinaryNode`, along with a new one `BinarySearchTree`. Take a look at them now, if you have not done so already.

Modifying BinaryTree with Parent References

The binary tree with parent pointers will be the starting point for this lab. If you did not do the last lab, this section has the necessary instructions to add in parent references.

To skip this section, copy the final versions of BinaryNode and BinaryTree from the last lab into the TreePackage folder. Change BinaryTree so that it implements BinaryTreeInterface and then skip ahead to step 10.

Step 1. In the class `BinaryNode`, add a private variable that will hold the parent reference.

Step 2. Add a new constructor that has four arguments: `data`, `left`, `right`, and `parent`.

Step 3. Modify the constructor that takes three arguments to use the new constructor.

Step 4. Create and fully implement three new methods in `BinaryNode`:
```
public BinaryNodeInterface<T> getParent()
public void setParent(BinaryNodeInterface<T> p)
public boolean hasParent()
```

Checkpoint: Compile BinarySearchTree, BinaryNode and BinaryTree. All tests in TestBinaryTree and TestBST should pass.

Step 5. Make a duplicate of the method `copy()` in `BinaryNode` and add a single argument `BinaryNode<T>` p to the duplicate.

Step 6. In the duplicate, set the parent of `newRoot` to be p.

Step 7. In the original, set the parent of of `newRoot` to be parent. (We will assume that if the original version of the copy method is being called, it is the top of the tree being copied and the parent should be the same. The duplicate version of copy will be used for all other nodes in the copy.)

Step 8. In both the original and the duplicate, change the two recursive calls to `copy()` so that they pass `newRoot` as the parameter.

Checkpoint: BinaryNode should compile successfully.

Checkpoint: Compile BinaryNode and BinaryTree. All tests in TestBinaryTree and TestBasicAccess should still pass.

The modification of BinaryNode is finished. The next goal is to modify BinaryTree appropriately. Any time a new binary tree is created, parent references for children may need to be set.

Step 9. Anywhere in `BinaryTree` that a left or right child is set, set a parent reference in an appropriate fashion. Since `BinaryNodeInterface<T>` does not have the methods for accessing the parent, a cast to `BinaryNode<T>` will be required.

Checkpoint: Compile BinaryNode and BinaryTree. All tests in TestBinaryTree and TestBasicAccess should still pass.

Threading the BinaryTree

Step 10. In the class `BinaryNode`, add a private variable that will hold the thread reference.

Step 11. Add a new constructor that has five arguments: `data`, `left`, `right`, `parent`, and `thread`.

Step 12. Modify the constructor that takes four arguments to use the new constructor.

Step 13. Create and fully implement three new methods in `BinaryNode`:
```
public BinaryNodeInterface<T> getThread()
public void setThread(BinaryNodeInterface<T> target)
public boolean hasThread()
```

Checkpoint: Compile BinarySearchTree, BinaryNode, and BinaryTree. All tests in TestBinaryTree and TestBST should still pass.

Step 14. Create and complete the method `linkSubtreeThreadOut ()` in `BinaryNode`. Refer to the Pre-Lab Exercises.

Step 15. In both of the `copy()` methods in `BinaryNode` make a call to `linkSubtreeThreadOut` to thread the left subtree to the root.

Step 16.   Create and complete the method getLeftmostInSubtree() in BinaryNode. Refer to the Pre-Lab Exercises.

Step 17.   In the both copy() methods in BinaryNode add code that will thread the root to the leftmost node in the right subtree.

Checkpoint: Compile BinarySearchTree, BinaryNode, and BinaryTree. All tests in TestBinaryTree and TestBST should still pass.

The modification of BinaryNode is finished. The next goal is to modify BinaryTree appropriately. Any time a new binary tree is created, threads for children may need to be set.

Step 18.   Anywhere in BinaryTree that a left child is set, set a thread reference for the subtree in an appropriate fashion. Since BinaryNodeInterface does not have the methods for accessing the thread/parent references, a cast to BinaryNode will be required.

Step 19.   Similarly, anywhere in BinaryTree that a right child is set, set a thread reference from the root to the leftmost node in the subtree in an appropriate fashion.

Checkpoint: Compile BinarySearchTree, BinaryNode, and BinaryTree. All tests in TestBinaryTree and TestBST should still pass.

It is now time to see if the threads work. The in-order iterator will be changed to use the threads.

Implementing an In-Order Iterator with Threads

Step 20.   In the class BinaryTree, create a copy of the private inner class InorderIterator. Comment out the original.

Step 21.   Remove the variable nodeStack. Now that threading is available, the stack will not be needed.

Step 22.   Refer to the Pre-Lab Exercises and create a private method in InorderIterator that will move the current node to the first node to be printed in an in-order traversal.

Step 23.   Call the new method in the constructor just after setting the currentNode to the root. (Make sure the root is not null before doing so though.)

Step 24.   Complete the hasNext() method.

Step 25.   Complete the next() method. It should be much simpler now. It just needs to remember the value to return and then move the current reference. Don't forget to throw NoSuchElementException when there are no more elements to be iterated over.

Checkpoint: Compile BinaryNode and BinaryTree. All tests in TestBinaryTree should still pass.

This is the first real test of the threading. To debug the code, it may be helpful to print whenever a node is created (along with the data) and to print whenever a thread is set. When finished, comment out the print statements. They may be useful in the next section.

Now it is time to make sure that BinarySearchTree respects parent references and threads.

Threading the BinarySearchTree

Step 26. Anywhere in the add() method of `BinarySearchTree` that a left or right child is set, parent references and threads must be adjusted. Refer to the Pre-Lab Exercises.

Checkpoint: Compile `BinarySearchTree`. All the tests except for remove should pass.

Step 27. Anywhere in the `removeNode()` method of `BinarySearchTree` that a left or right child is set or the root is changed, parent references and threads must be adjusted. Refer to the Pre-Lab Exercises. (Of all the methods that collaberate to perform the remove, the only method that affects the structure of the tree is removeNode, so it is the only one where references might need to change.)

Checkpoint: Compile `BinarySearchTree`. All the tests in `TestBST` should pass.

Getting Identifiers from a Java Program

Step 1. The application `Identifiers` exists but needs to be completed.

Step 2. Copy *Small.java* and *X.java* to the default directory that Java's runtime environment uses.

Checkpoint: The application should run. Enter file name X.java. The program will open the file for reading then quit.

Step 3. In the method `getPossibleIds()` in `Identifiers` create a loop to read lines from the file.

Step 4. In the loop, read a line using the Scanner input and use it to create a StringTokenizer.

Step 5. Create another loop that uses the `StringTokenizer` to get tokens and place them in the binary search tree. (Use a string of delimeters that includes any character that would mark the end of a token. For example, in the code x+=y*eff; each of the symbols +, * and ; mark the end of an identifier.)

Step 6. In the main, use an in-order iterator to print out the values in the binary search tree.

Final checkpoint: The application should run. Enter file name X.java. The list of identifiers should be a b c d e ef g.

Run the application again. Enter file name Small.java. This is a very short working java application. The list of possible identifiers should be in alphabetical order and should correctly include the identifiers in the program.

Test the application on other Java files.

Post-Lab Follow Ups

1. Create a new implementation of a threaded binary search tree that uses two thread references, one to the in-order predecessor and the other to the in-order successor. Do not use a parent reference.

2. Create a new implementation of a threaded binary search tree that uses circular references for the threads. (The last node in an in-order traversal threads back to the first node.)

3. Design and implement a recursive version of the method `linkSubtreeThreadOut()` in `BinaryNode`.

4. Design and implement a recursive version of the method `getLeftmostInSubtree()` in `BinaryNode`.

5. Modify the `Identifiers` application to ignore any text in comments or string constants.

6. Modify the `Identifiers` application to use a second binary search tree that holds Java keywords. Do not add keywords to the list of identifiers.

7. Create a new implementation of a threaded binary search tree that uses thread references, but instead of having the threads give an in-order traversal, create a level-order traversal.

8. An alternate version of a binary search tree allows multiple copies of the same value in the tree. The search tree property will allow equal value nodes in either sub-tree. When adding a duplicate value into the tree, randomly choose a sub-tree of the original value. This will help prevent imbalanced trees. When removing a value from the tree, remove the first copy found.

    Develop and implement this alternate version of a binary search tree. The test classes will need to be changed for the new definition.

Appendix A: Animation Framework

Animated Application

This appendix describes the framework used by a number of the labs to implement an animated application. This framework supports applications that have a set up phase where application specific variables are set. The application then runs and has checkpoints that the user can step between where the state of the application is displayed graphically. The application can be reset at any point and restarted. Note that this framework is not designed to handle applications like games that periodically require user input, but an experienced programmer could modify it to do so.

Instead of just giving the framework with blanks to be filled in by the programmer, a simple application demonstrating the framework is shown. It computes the terms of an arithmetic sequence.

The Framework

The following class diagram shows the relationship among the classes in the application. The classes that are shaded are the specific classes that implement the application. The other classes are the framework classes.

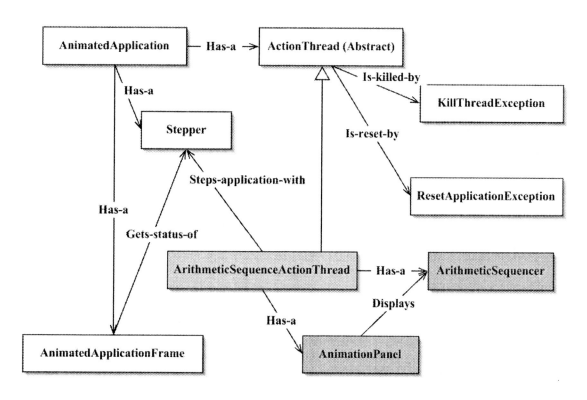

AnimatedApplication

This class has the `main()` method used to invoke the application. It is responsible for creating

1. an `AnimatedApplicationFrame`, which contains the controls for stepping the application,

2. a `Stepper`, which is how the application will signal that it is waiting, and

3. an `ActionThread` that executes the application.

Once these objects are created, `main` starts the `ActionThread`. This is the only class in the framework that needs to change for different applications. (An action thread of the appropriate type needs to be created.)

Stepper

This class acts as an intermediary between the control components of the frame and application. It has a number of methods where the action thread can wait for a step to occur. The state of the action thread (setup phase, initial phase, stepping, final phase) will be indicated by the specific call that gets made. The animation frame will set the controls based on the state of the stepper. When stepping, the stepper will keep track of the step that the application is on.

> `getStep()`—This method is used by the application frame when displaying the controls. It returns the number of application steps since the last reset.
>
> `getStatus()`—This method is used by the application frame when displaying the controls. It returns what kind the wait step was.
>
> `setupStep()`—This method will be used by the action thread. It will change the status of the stepper and then wait for notification it can continue. It should only be used to indicate that the application specific controls can be used to set the parameters for the application.
>
> `initialStateStep()`—This method is used by the action thread. It will change the status of the stepper and then wait for notification it can continue. This step occurs after initialization has been performed for the application, but the application has yet to start running.
>
> `animationStep()`—This method is used by the action thread. It will change the status of the stepper and then wait for notification it can continue. These steps are counted and are the actual steps in the execution of the application.
>
> `finalStep()`—This method is used by the action thread. It will change the status of the stepper and then wait for notification it can continue. In this step the application has finished execution and the final state of the animation display is held so it can be viewed.

It is not intended that the application thread interact directly with the stepper, but instead will use methods defined in the abstract class `ActionThread` to affect the stepper.

This class should not be changed for new applications.

AnimatedApplicationFrame

This class is subclass of `JFrame` and holds the entire application. It creates the user interface components for stepping the application. The control components are placed in a panel, which in turn is placed in the north position of the frame. The specific animation panel for the application is retrieved from the action thread and placed in the center position of the frame. This class will use a `Timer` that fires and generates a step at given intervals. The timer will be started if go is pressed. It will be stopped if pause or reset is pressed. A step will notify the waiting action thread that it can continue.

This class should not need to be changed for new applications.

ActionThread

This abstract class specifies certain responsibilities that an `ActionThread` must satisfy to "play nicely" with the `AnimatedApplicationFrame`. The major responsibilities of an `actionThread` are to

1. define the general run method for executing the thread,

2. have a stepper object to control the animation,

3. have a panel that the application will do its animation on, and

4. have a mechanism to kill or reset the thread.

The heart of the ActionThread class is the run() method.

> run()—Any thread must define this method to specify what happens when the thread is executed. For the ActionThread class, the thread will execute the application of interest one or more times. There will be a setup phase, where the user is allowed to change the input parameters for the application. The application will be initialized and then executed. There is a final step, which allows the final state of the application to be displayed. It is not intended that this method be modified.

The ActionThread class has some methods that its subclasses can use when implementing the animation

> animationPause()—This method should be called any time that the state of the application has changed and the animation needs to be updated. It automatically calls makeThreadWellBehaved(). It is not intended that this method be modified.

> forceLastPause()—If you want to kill or reset the animation, an exception needs to be thrown. Before invoking the exception, you should do an animation pause. This method will indicate that the animation should go to the last step and it should be called before the exception is thrown. It is not intended that this method be modified.

> makeThreadWellBehaved()—Because of the cooperative technique that Java uses to kill a thread (explained below) the thread should regularly check to see if it needs to kill itself. It is automatically as part of every animation pause. If there is a part of the application that is computationally intensive, it is a good idea to call this function throughout the computation. It is not intended that this method be modified.

> getAnimationPanel()—Get the panel that is holding the application specific animation. It is not intended that this method be modified.

> applicationControlsAreActive()—Returns true if the animation is in the setup phase and the application specific controls should be active. It is not intended that this method be modified.

As an abstract class, ActionThread specifies some methods that are the responsibility of its specific subclasses to implement. These are related to the general mechanism for executing the thread.

> getApplicationTitle()—Return the title of this application.

> createAnimationPanel()—Create and return the panel that the application will do its animation on.

> setUpApplicationSpecificControls()—Create all of the components and panels for the user interface for the application. Place them on the animation panel. (Use the getAnimationPanel() method.)

> Since the panel will also be used to display the animation, you should be careful about where the components are placed. It is probably best to leave the center free. Placing the controls on the right side or the bottom may also make it easier to draw the animation. Creating the handlers for the controls can be done in a number of different ways. One fairly typical technique (which is used in the example) is to create an anonymous inner class that acts as a listener for the component. It calls a handler method, which is easier to locate than code embedded in the inner class.

> init()—This method will be run before the application is executed in the setup phase. It will initialize any variables that the application will use.

> executeApplication()—A method that does a single execution of the application. The entire code for the application may be contained within this method, but it is not required. In fact, good program design encourages abstraction via the creation of other methods. For thread safety, the application should never change or access any of the components in the

user interface. Instead, it will change display variables. The display will be redrawn using the new status of the display variables when the `animationPause()` method is invoked.

One of the requirements is that the application that is being run should be killable. The approved technique in Java is to use cooperative action. The outside object, which wishes to kill the thread, calls a method that sets a variable. Periodically the thread must check this variable and if needed kill itself.

The thread that is created will run the application one or more times. This necessitates the ability to reset the application in the thread. Using cooperative action, a variable will be set. As before, the thread is responsible for checking periodically to see if it needs to be reset.

> `resetExecution()`—Allow an outside object to signal this thread to reset the application it is currently running.

> `killThread()`—Allow an outside object to signal this thread to kill itself.

ResetApplicationException

The `makeThreadWellBehaved()` method in `ActionThread` will throw this exception if the current execution of the application should be halted. It is caught by `run()` and appropriate action is taken. This class should not need to be changed for new applications.

KillThreadException

The `makeThreadWellBehaved()` method in `ActionThread` will throw this exception if the thread needs to die. It is caught by `run()` and appropriate action is taken. This class should not need to be changed for new applications.

The Arithmetic Sequence Application

There are three classes that implement the application that computes arithmetic sequences. These three classes are specific to the sample application, but they can serve as a model for the creation of new applications. One issue that must be addressed in these classes is thread safety.

Thread Safety

The animated application will have two threads running concurrently. One thread will be the application that is being executed and the other will be a thread that deals with the graphical user interface. Problems can occur when both threads can access a shared object. If the object is mutable, a situation can arise where one thread starts to change the state of the object and then is interrupted by the thread manager. If the second thread accesses the object, it can be in an invalid state. If both threads mutate the object, they can interfere with one another in unpredictable ways.

ArithmeticSequenceActionThread

This class is a concrete subclass of `ActionThread` and has the primary responsibility of defining how the arithmetic sequence application operates. The major work in using the framework for a different application lies in creating a class like this.

There are two kinds of private variables that an application will typically have. The first kind of variable will be referred to as a parameter of the application. These variables can be changed by the user interface of the application in the setup phase. They are then used to initialize any private variables that the application needs to run. They should not be changed during the running of the application. Examples of this kind of variable in the arithmetic sequence application are `start` and `delta`. These variables should always be initialized when they are declared.

The second kind of variable will be referred to as display variables. They are variables that will affect the graphics display of the animation. Display variables can be accessed by both of the threads in the animated application so thread safety is an issue. They should either be primitives, immutable, or specially designed objects. Examples of this kind of variable in the sample application are `mySequencer` and `count`. The responsibilities of the specially designed objects will be shown later with the `ArithmeticSequencer` class.

Since `ArithmeticSequenceActionThread` is a concrete subclass of `ActionThread`, it must define the abstract methods of `ActionThread`. These methods are specialized for the arithmetic sequence application:

> `getApplicationTitle()`—Returns "Arithmetic Sequences (Sample Application)".

> `createAnimationPanel()`—Creates and returns a new `AnimationPanel`.

> `setUpApplicationSpecificControls()`—Creates and places two text fields on the animation panel, one for the initial value in the sequence and the other for the difference between terms in the sequence. Creates and places three labels on the animation panel.

> `init()`—Initializes all the variables that the application needs to execute. It will be invoked immediately after the setup phase and may use the application parameters to initialize the other variables. In the arithmetic sequence application, there are just the two display variables, `count` and `mySequencer`, that need to be initialized.

> `executeApplication()`—A method that does a single execution of the application. It contains a loop that runs ten times. The body of the loop adds the next term in the sequence using the `mySeqencer` object and then pauses the animation.

The class has two handler methods for the text fields. Thread safety is an issue with these methods since they will be invoked from the user interface thread. The handlers should only change the parameters for the application. In addition, only the handlers are allowed to access the user interface components.

> `countByTextFieldHandler()`—A handler method that gets the string from the `countByTextField`, converts the string into an integer, and then initializes the `count` parameter.

> `startAtTextFieldHandler()`—A handler method that gets the string from the `startAtTextField`, converts the string into an integer, and then initializes the `start` parameter.

To be really well behaved, the handlers should only change the parameters if the application is in the setup phase. The method `applicationControlsAreActive()` can be used to check if the application is in the setup phase.

The application thread (any methods that are invoked from `executeApplication()`) should not access any of the user interface components, as they are not thread safe.

AnimationPanel

It is expected that every subclass of `ActionThread` will have an inner class that has the single responsibility to draw the animation frame. Thread safety is a concern, so it should only access display variables.

> `paintComponent()`—This method draws the animation frame. It must call the super class method first. This guarantees that any components on the panel are drawn. It is expected that specially designed display classes will do most of the actual drawing. Before drawing, it is important to check that any nonprimitive display variables are nonnull.

> For the arithmetic sequence application, the number of terms added from the sequence is drawn in a string. If `mySequencer` has been initialized, it will draw itself on the panel.

ArithmeticSequencer

The display variable `mySequencer` is of this type. It is a specialized auxiliary class that holds information that will be displayed by the application during the animation. This kind of class will have mutator methods that the application calls.

> `addNext()`—A mutator that directs the object to compute the next term in the sequence. A string with that term will be added to the list of terms that will be displayed.

The other responsibility of this kind of class is to draw a representation of itself on a given graphics context.

> `drawOn()`—This method draws on the given graphics context. Besides the graphics context, it often will have as parameters *x* and *y* coordinates that shift the origin of what it draws. It may also have a scale parameter that changes the size of the drawing.
>
> For the `ArithmeticSequencer` application, a star like object will be drawn with one spoke for each of the terms computed so far. Each of the strings will then be displayed, one to a line. (Each will have a term in the sequence.)

These auxiliary animation classes are shared by both the application thread (mutator methods) and the user interface thread (the `drawOn()` method). Therefore, thread safety is important. All methods in the auxiliary display classes should be synchronized.

Using the Framework to Create New Applications

The following is offered as a guideline for using the framework to create a new animated application. It uses the arithmetic sequence application as a starting point.

Preparation

Step 1.   Decide on a name for your application. (The name will be referred to as XXXX in the rest of the guidelines.)

Step 2.   What information must your application have before it can start? Only list those things that the user can change.

Examples are

> **numerical values**—such as the size of an array or number of values to generate
>
> **strings**—such as the name of a file containing data
>
> **Boolean values**—such as a flag indicating the amount of information to be displayed
>
> **Enumerations**—such as the color of a displayed component

Step 3.   What should be displayed at each step of the animation? Create rough sketches.

Step 4.   Is the animation display composed of pieces? Write down class names for each of the pieces (auxiliary classes). (These are analogous to `ArithmeticSequencer` in the sample application.) Give a brief list of responsibilities of these classes. Think carefully about the states that the classes can be in. List methods that change the state of these classes.

Step 5.   Copy the files in the *Arithmetic Sequence* folder into a new folder.

Step 6.   Make a copy of `ArithmeticSequenceActionThread` and call it `XXXXActionThread`. Change the class declaration and the constructor to match the new name for the class.

Step 7.   Make a copy of `AnimatedApplication` and call it `XXXXApplication`. Change the class declaration to match.

Changes to AnimatedApplication

Step 8. Change the creation of myThread to use XXXXThread instead of ArithmeticSequenceActionThread.

At this point, no more changes are needed to XXXXApplication. Before working on the action thread, it is a good idea to create the auxiliary classes that will be used to draw the animation. The class ArithmeticSequencer can be used as a model.

Auxiliary Animation Classes

Step 9. Create each of the auxiliary classes listed earlier.

Step 10. Create constructors for each class.

Step 11. Create the accessor methods for each of the classes.

Step 12. Create the mutator methods for each of the classes.

Step 13. Create a drawOn() method for each class. This class must have a parameter Graphics g, which is the context that the class will draw itself on. It is strongly recommended that a position (*x* and *y* coordinates) be passed in as well that the drawing will be relative to. A scale parameter may also be useful.

Step 14. Test the auxiliary classes. These tests do not need to be exhaustive and do not need to test drawOn.

Remember to make all the methods of these classes **synchronized** so they are thread safe.

The major changes will be to the action thread. These changes will be approached in small chunks. First the arithmetic sequence applications code will be cleared to make way for the new application. Keep the original code in comments so it can be referred to if needed.

Clearing Out the Code in XXXXThread

Step 15. Comment out the declaration of the private variables start and delta that were parameters for the application.

Step 16. Comment out the declaration of the private variables mySequencer and count that were display variables for the application.

Step 17. Comment out the body of the methods init(), executeApplication(), and paintComponent() of the inner class AnimationPanel.

XXXXThread should compile with no errors. The next change to make is to add in the application specific controls.

Creating the Application-Specific Control Components

Step 18. Refer back to your preparations and create a private variable for each parameter (required piece of information to start the application). Put them in the place of the declarations for start and delta. Make sure that they are initialized.

Step 19. Create user interface components for each of the parameters to allow them to be set. The arithmetic sequence application puts all of the components into a panel named setupPanel, which it puts in the south location of the animation panel. More panels can be used and other locations used as desired. Do not put anything in the center, since that will be used for displaying the animation.

Step 20. Use the existing code as a template for setting up the listeners for each of the components. Create handler methods for each of the components. (Use the existing handlers as examples.) Make sure the handlers set the appropriate private variables and provide feedback via the setupStatusLabel.

XXXXThread should compile with no errors and the application should run. Check that the application specific controls operate. The next change will be to initialize the application and make sure that the animation is displayed correctly.

Initialization of the Application

Step 21. Change the title returned by getApplicationTitle().

Step 22. Create variables for the items that will be displayed graphically by the application. (These go where mySequencer and count were.)

Step 23. Initialize each of the variables that were just created in the init() method.

Step 24. Add code to the paintComponent() method, which will draw each of the pieces. Most of the time this will involve calling drawOn() methods for the specific objects. Two notes: First, make sure that super.paintComponent(g) is called. The component will not draw correctly without it. Second, this method may be called before init() has had a chance to work. So before using any object, make sure that it is nonnull.

XXXXThread should compile with no errors and the application should run. Set the variables and then click on Step. The initial state of the application should be displayed. Debug the code as needed so that the display is correct. If needed, you can add calls to the mutators for the display variables in init() and verify the displays and methods work as expected.

Stepping the Application

Step 25. Add in code to executeApplication() that specifies what the application is to do. Create new methods as needed. Create new private variables as needed. As with any project, it is a good idea to work incrementally.

Whenever you want the application to change its display, add in the following line of code.

```
animationPause();
```

This will make the application wait until it is stepped (either manually, or after a given delay if the go button has been pressed). It also makes the thread well behaved (checks to see if the application thread should be killed or reset).

If you have sections of the code that are computationally intensive (do not make many calls to animationPause()), it is a good idea to add extra calls to makeThreadWellBehaved(). For example, it can be placed in the body of an iteration or recursive function.